Coping
with
Difficult Teachers

Coping
with
Difficult Teachers

by

Angela V. Woodhull, Ph.D.

SCHENKMAN BOOKS, INC.
ROCHESTER, VERMONT

Copyright © 1996

Allen County Public Library
900 Webster Street
PO Box 2270
Fort Wayne, IN 46801-2270

Schenkman Books, Inc.
118 Main Street
Rochester, Vermont 05767

Library of Congress Cataloging-in-Publication Data

Woodhull, Angela Victoria, 1950–
    Coping with difficult teachers/Angela V. Woodhull.
    p.   cm.
    Includes bibliographical references.
    ISBN 0-87047-102-3
    1. Teacher-student relationships. 2. High school teachers—
Attitudes. 3. College teachers—Attitudes. 4. Communication
in education. 5. Sexual Harassment in education.   I. Title
    LB 1033.W66   1995
    371. 1'023—dc20   95-36255
                                                    CIP

Printed in the United States of America

Contents

Foreword

Students who feel defenseless and alone in battling unreasonable instructors, who seem hell-bent on making their lives unduly stressful, will find that the advice and communication strategies offered in *Coping With Difficult Teachers* will assist them in achieving fair treatment without appearing overbearing or disrespectful.

It's frustrating to make an appointment to meet a professor in his office, then be stood up by a no-show. It's infuriating to study class notes, then be stumped by test questions that were never covered in the text or discussed in class by the instructor. It's embarrassing to be purposely humiliated by a teacher for daring to ask a challenging question. Dr. Woodhull gives students concrete examples of how to combat these problems, presented in lively, inviting anecdotes that will make students want to read more.

As the publisher of several nationally distributed student-oriented magazines*, I've seen and heard horror stories of how a few instructors and professors have used and abused students in their classes; how they've unethically taken advantage of the students' inexperience and reluctance to protest too loudly for fear of reprisal; how they've played favorites; and how they have given grades or evaluations based on the students' response to their unwanted sexual advances. Chapter 13 of this book on dealing with sexual harassment is particularly timely and useful.

Coping With Difficult Teachers is a sure winner. I highly recommend it for any student who wants to be a campus leader.

W.H. "Butch" Oxendine, Jr.
President, Oxendine Publishing, Inc.

---

* Oxendine Publishing, Inc. is publisher of *Florida Leader*, *Student Leader*, *Careers & Majors*, and *Transfer Student*.

Introduction

DIFFICULT TEACHERS! AUGH!!!

What picture comes to mind when you hear the words *difficult teachers*? For some students it's the image of a teacher with thick glasses standing in front of the classroom, mumbling boring passages straight out of a textbook. For others, it's teachers who bristle when a student asks a simple question. They snap, "Didn't I already answer that question at least a dozen times!?" In the words of a high school sophomore, "Its some psycho who sits behind his desk reading a book on stress management and then he looks up and screams at the class."

It's burdensome enough that you have three finals tomorrow and now the instructor wants you to memorize five thousand obscure ancient Sanskrit terms? Then, when she passes out the test, she announces, "I've changed my mind about what's on the exam. No Sanskrits. Those of you who studied everything will do fine." I call this personality type of difficult teacher *Crazy-making Double Binders*. Difficult teachers can make you twitch uncomfortably when you think about your final grade.

A study conducted in the early eighties asked the question, "What's in a grade?" (Hughey and Harper 1983, ERIC System*). The conclusion? A student's communication style has quite a big influence on the final grade. How the student interacts and communicates with a teacher, along with the stereotypes the student fits, accounts for 16 percent of how the final grade is determined!

---

*The ERIC System, which stands for "Educational Resources Informational Center" is a federally funded information system designed to provide users with ready access to an extensive body of educational-related materials, including reports, conference proceedings, and journal articles. Established in 1966, ERIC is supported by the U.S. Department of Education, Office of Educational Reasearch and Improvement.

... to get a high grade in the course, it is best to be a female*
with a lenient instructor. It is best to work on preventing
communication problems, to impose coherence upon communication encounters, to talk in an adaptive way, and to seek
understanding from these encounters. Being a 'listens-to-
anything' kind of listener is an advantage.

It's an inescapable fact of academic life that some teachers are going to
be difficult. But when a difficult teacher is making your life miserable,
you needn't resort to dropping courses, or taking Socrates' way out—and
drink the fatal hemlock!

This book is designed to help high school and college students cope
with difficult teachers by learning the necessary communication skills.
How well you communicate *does* affect your final grade. So, what's in a
grade? Only your academic transcript, your career, and possibly your future.

---

*In chapter 10, however, you will learn the *hazards* of being female in academia, especially
in graduate school.

PART I

Recognizing and Communicating with Difficult Teachers

1

Five General Principles of Communication

The best way to start coping more effectively with difficult teachers is to practice five general principles of effective communication. A general principle is a rule that can be applied to more than one situation. The foil method that students learn in Algebra I is an example of a general principle. Students use the foil method to solve any algebraic equation that fits the pattern $(a \pm b) \times (c \pm d)$.

The Benefits of Learning General Principles of Communication

A few rare students have a natural ability for getting along with difficult teachers, but they can't articulate what it is they are doing that works so well. Most students do not have such a knack. Learning the five basic communication principles helps students to be clearly cognizant of communication techniques that work well.

Poor communicators generally feel defeated when they encounter difficult teachers. They lament:

"When a situation is getting tense, I open my mouth and generally make things worse."

"I might as well not say anything at all."

"Nobody gets along with him, so I might as well not even try."

Effective communicators, on the other hand, experience a sense of personal power. They think before they speak, listen effectively, and use diplomacy when telling others what they want and expect. Let's begin now by examining the five general principles of effective communication.

FIVE GENERAL PRINCIPLES OF EFFECTIVE COMMUNICATION

- Begin a transaction in a friendly manner.

- Be friendly but not familiar.

- Communicate in the adult ego state.

- Synergize.

- Dress professionally (so you won't fit the negative stereotypes).

Let's examine each of these principles in more detail.

Begin a transaction in a friendly manner. It is important to begin a conversation on a positive note. Begin with a smile, the first sign of genuine friendliness. Why is a smile so important? Think of the last time you went shopping or went out to dinner. Did the waiter or clerk begin with a smile? Have you ever been stopped for speeding? The traffic officer set the tone by the way he began the transaction. Some motorists become difficult when they are approached in an unfriendly manner. When communicating with a difficult teacher, your smile is a way of saying, "I'm here to work things out. We're not enemies."

Tone of voice also carries the message of friendliness. I know a man who speaks to everyone in a very gruff tone. One day, someone asked, "Hey Charlie, why do you always sound so mad?" Charlie yelled, "That's a stupid question! I'm not mad!!!"

Your tone of voice lets the listener know what mood you're in. Your words won't impact a difficult teacher as much if you sound mad, frightened, irritated, or sad. Learn to speak in a tone that says, "I'm positive and I'm professional. I believe in myself and I'm proud of who I am." Think to yourself, "I'm proud. PROUD. Proud and friendly." When you're mustering up the courage to approach a difficult teacher, your words will have a much greater impact.

Be friendly, but not familiar. What's the difference? Familiar students talk about their own personal life and problems. They send signals to difficult teachers that can be misinterpreted. Friendly students talk about subjects that relate to school. By sticking to business, they let difficult teachers know they're not available to be victimized.

Communicate in the Adult Ego State. There are three ways people can represent themselves when they are communicating: as a child, a parent, or an adult. These three personifications are known as ego states. Let's look at some examples of each of the three ego states.

CHILD EGO STATE

A person speaking from their child ego state sounds defensive, trapped, and victimized. Here's what a student relating from the child ego state might sound like:

"Why is she always picking on me?"

"It's hopeless. I can't do anything about this situation."

"I wish I could change her, but she won't listen to me."

"He makes me feel so bad."

"I wish that teacher would change her attitude!"

"Why even bother to study? His tests never make any sense."

"I might as well just flunk."

Wishing, hoping, and *feeling* that "it's no use" are typical ways in which people in the child ego state express themselves. They also use words like "never" and "always."

PARENT EGO STATE

Like the child ego state, a person doesn't have to be a parent to come across like a parent. A person speaking from the parent ego state sounds authoritarian and bossy. They feel they have the right to tell others what to do, how to think, and how to feel. Here's what a student talking to a teacher from the parent ego state might sound like:

"You are wasting our time by giving us all of this ridiculous homework."

"You need to learn how to teach."

"I'm going to make sure I get you in trouble for this."

"You need to change your attitude."

"The class doesn't think you're teaching this right, so here's what we've decided to do."

"I can't believe you said that to me in front of the entire class. You have no right to do that."

Notice the difference between the child and the parent ego states. The child feels helpless, so he doesn't bother to speak. The parent feels too much power. By addressing others in an authoritarian manner, they make others feel hostile and defensive. They feel they have a right to make decisions that affect other people without consulting them.

ADULT EGO STATE

People who talk in the adult ego state sound self-confident, positive, and self-sufficient. They think well of others. They don't try to put people down. Their tone of voice sounds warm and friendly. They consult before making decisions that affect others.

Another characteristic of people who speak from the adult ego state is that they talk in "information mode." In other words, they stick to issues rather than wage personal attack statements. Let's examine the difference:

Statements of Personal Attack

- You give us too much work to do! You should stop assigning all that work because we have other classes, too!

- You have no right to talk to me like that!

Information Mode

- Mr. Frazier, I'd like to speak to you about our group project. I've analyzed the amount of time that will be needed to sufficiently complete our report. Here are my findings.

- Dr. Smith, I'd like more information. In class you mentioned that my ideas are irrelevant and uninteresting. Could you give me a further explanation?

I witnessed a stewardess speaking in *information mode* to a difficult passenger who refused to put up his tray. He remained oblivious to her requests. But instead of talking to him in a bossy, authoritarian, parental way ("I said you need to put up that tray right now! Federal regulations say so!"), she kept repeating a very simple message every time she passed him. Pointing gently to the tray, she said, "That tray needs to come up." A few minutes later, she delivered the same, friendly message, "That tray needs to come up." After a third try, the stewardess succeeded in getting the man to put up the tray. She spoke to him in information mode and stuck to the issue of the tray rather than using the pronoun *you*.

Like the professional stewardess, students who address difficult teachers in information mode are more likely to get what they want.

Synergize. Every problem has more than one solution. Synergy means "cooperative interaction between two forms." A student who learns how to synergize can see many ways to make a bad situation better. When dealing with a difficult teacher, students who practice the principle of synergy know they can:

- Talk to the teacher in information mode

- Switch to another class

- Talk with the dean or principal

- Seek help from other sources besides the teacher, such as librarians, tutors, parents, other students, encyclopedias and other reference sources

- Lodge a formal complaint

- Appeal to higher authorities

- Talk to their parents

- Petition with other students

- Change their own perceptions

- Consult with an attorney

- Accept and adapt.

Synergy is like playing with a Rubic's Cube. If the current pattern doesn't work, twist and turn the pieces until you find the pattern that *does*.

Students who synergize are resourceful; they know that there's more than one way to tackle a problem. They realize that the teacher is probably not going to change, and that they cannot change the teacher, so they take action to make things better in their own life, rather than just whining and complaining.

Dress professionally (so you won't fit the image of a sloppy, "do-the-minimum" kind of student). People really do judge others by appearance. In his book, *Supervisor's Factomatic* (1986), Jack Horn lists in Appendix Z, a "Checklist of Items that will Kill a Career in Supervision Fast"). Item number 17 reads, "Dress and groom slovenly. Don't judge a book by its cover is your attitude." College and high school are both testing grounds for the world of work. The habits you cultivate while in school will affect your future career. Teachers judge students by their appearance and they are more likely to give favorable job references and higher grades to students who dress professionally. Ms. Donna Gavin, Director of the Barbizon School of Modeling, said:

> We stress how important personal appearance is because people make their first impressions based upon appearance. Professional appearance is a total package. It means being well-groomed, but its also everything that affects how a person feels about himself or herself. We also emphasize posture—how people carry themselves, which affects the attitudes of others. People with good posture, who walk with a confident attitude, are going to feel good about themselves, and others are going to recognize that. People want to be around confident-looking people who look like they're having fun. It makes a person more likeable.

> I believe teachers have a better impression of a person who's well put together. The polished person is more respected.

> A person with poor posture, sloppily dressed gives the first impression that he/she generally doesn't care about himself/ herself. A negative first impression generally means a person has to work harder to prove himself. But the person who is polished has the advantage of a favorable first impression.

FROM DEPENDENCE TO INDEPENDENCE

Effective communicators are independent. They rely on themselves to get things done. Here's what some students said after practicing the five general principles of effective communication.

> "It no longer matters to me if the teacher likes me. I'm here to get an education and to make sure I am treated fairly. If I'm not treated fairly, I'll do something about it."

> "The teacher still has the ultimate say-so, but I also have the power to decide how I am going to react."

> "When I feel sad for too long, I know it's time for me to take responsibility and change my own mood."

> "I realize I cannot wait for the teacher to change. By changing my own attitude, I am no longer a target for difficult teachers."

In the following chapters you'll learn how effective communicators apply the five general principles to cope with difficult teachers and ultimately get better grades!

2

Apathetic Teachers: Ms. Apathy and Mr. Unconcerned

Let's begin by examining a pair of teachers you'd rather do without—*Ms. Apathy* and *Mr. Unconcerned*. Ms. Apathy assigns a lot of busy work, which she never grades. Mr. Unconcerned always has a very placid look on his face. The only time he shows any facial expression is when a student approaches him with a question, when he rolls his eyes and sighs heavily. Yesterday, you saw Mr. Unconcerned drive up to the school two minutes before the final bell. You noticed his bumper sticker—"I'd rather be fishing"—as he exited his vehicle, yawning.

In this chapter, we'll look at five types of apathetic teachers:

- Teachers who don't answer students' questions sufficiently.

- Teachers who assign unproductive busy work.

- Teachers who give insufficient explanations.

- Teachers who never seem to want to help.

- Teachers who are boring and robotic.

TEACHERS WHO DON'T ANSWER STUDENTS' QUESTIONS SATISFACTORILY

Bruce was having difficulty understanding how to solve a math problem. Other than this one problem, he was doing fine in the class and held a B average. He went to the teacher's office and asked for help. The teacher wrote down the answer to the problem and said, "You figure it out from there."

How Bruce Sees The Problem

I was just asking him about one problem. It wasn't like I was asking him to explain the entire course! He could have explained how to do it without acting so apathetic! If he would only give me some hints, I would catch on.

How the Teacher Sees It

I'm so sick and tired of students asking me questions about things I've already covered sufficiently in class! Why wasn't he paying attention when I covered this information for the past three days in my lectures?! These students rely too much on me. They want to be pampered. They don't want to do their part. They need to learn how to get the answers on their own. If I were to take time to answer every student's question, I wouldn't have time for anything else. I'm already overworked. I am responsible for 150 students this semester. Imagine if each and everyone of them demanded 10 minutes of my time every day!

How to Handle It

Your goal is to get your questions answered. Try consulting other resources before approaching an apathetic teacher. The apathetic teacher already feels overburdened. You can consult the library, reference books, other students, your notes, or a tutor. Use a homework hotline if your town has one.

If you've already consulted all of the above and still can't get the answer, approach the teacher. The teacher will be more willing to answer your question if he feels that you have made an effort to seek the answer on your own.

Student: Mr. Brown, I'm wondering if I could take ten minutes of your time so you could answer a question for me. I've already checked my old textbooks, my class notes, my current textbook, fellow classmates, and a tutor, but no one knows how to work out this problem. I realize you covered this in class, but this problem still baffles me. It isn't like me to ask for help, and I know you are very busy, but I would really appreciate your help with this one problem.

Bravo for Bruce! He (1) told the teacher up front what he wanted without beating around the bush, (2) asked for a specific amount of time, (3) explained that he'd already consulted other resources, (4) gave proper authority to the teacher, and (5) showed appreciation. Even an apathetic teacher should feel inspired to help.

Some students become magnets for difficult teachers. They whine, complain, and continue to ask for help from stonewall teachers, or they just give up and stop asking questions. "It's no use. I'll just go ahead and flunk since the teacher won't help me."

Don't be a target for difficult teachers. When you need more information you can:

- Go to the library.

- Ask another student.

- Hire a tutor.

- Ask your parents, friends, or neighbors for help.

- Consult a librarian.

- Look it up in the encyclopedia or other reference books.

- Ask a teacher who enjoys helping students.

- Re-read your notes or textbook and try to figure it out. Sometimes, just a little more investigation helps you see the solution.

Students who realize they have lots of options available to them besides the teacher feel more powerful. They take learning seriously and stop focusing on the difficult teacher's flaws.

TEACHERS WHO ASSIGN UNPRODUCTIVE BUSY WORK

The teacher told Judy and the rest of the students to write thirty words and their definitions ten times each. While Judy wrote each word over and over again, she thought about the weekend football game, her boyfriend, and try-outs for the school play.

How Judy Sees the Problem

This assignment is ridiculous. After I write each word and definition ten times, I'm still going to have to go back and really learn each word for the test. This is so silly. And I probably will never even use any of these stupid words.

How the Teacher Sees It

Students don't realize how important it is to build their vocabulary. People who are well versed in the English language pass entrance examinations with higher scores, comprehend much more of what they read, and sound more intelligent when they speak. I'm showing them how to add piquancy and verve to their vocabulary! Repetition is the only way to learn.

How Not to Handle It

What do you suppose would happen if Judy approached the teacher like this?

Judy: Ms. Schaffer, I read a book on study skills that showed me a much better way to memorize words and definitions. The way you make us do things is boring and I never remember anything. I want to use my way, and so do the others.

The teacher will not listen to Judy. Enthusiasm cannot come across as a put-down.

How to Handle It

See the task in another way. Maybe the assignment really isn't so ridiculous. Try to see some benefit in what you're doing. Think of all the professionals who use their extensive vocabularies regularly. Nurses, doctors, teachers, writers, managers, police officers, and firefighters, to name a few, are required to use language skillfully in writing reports. Perhaps you, too, will be involved someday in a career that requires your proficiency in language.

Find an exciting new way to approach the homework. Some students use *mnemonics* to memorize new words and their definitions. Mnemonics is a technique to better remember something. The mnemonic device for remembering new words and definitions involves three steps: (1) Find a word you already know that reminds you of the new word. For example, let's say the new word is *catkin*, which is a cluster of flowers. A word you already know that reminds you of catkin is *cat.* (2) Associate your word reminder, cat, with the definition. Use visualization. You might picture a cat sniffing a cluster of flowers. (3) Your word reminder will help you remember your visual image the day of the test. You'll see the word *catkin* and remember—cat—and you'll recall your visual image of a cat sniffing a cluster of flowers. This picture helps you recall the definition of *catkin*. In university research, students who used mnemonics to remember words and definitions scored higher than students who learned the words by rote.

Tell the teacher about your exciting new way to learn the material. She may adopt the technique.

> *Judy:* Ms. Schaffer, I'm so excited about doing my words and definitions this week! I've discovered a new way to memorize words and definitions that really works for me! I'd like to use this technique to complete my homework. (Judy gives a demonstration.) Would you allow me to do my homework this way for the next two weeks? I'll draw pictures of my associations. And if my grades improve, will you let me use this technique permanently?

Judy is right on track! Her enthusiastic approach to learning will certainly pay off. She (1) began in a friendly manner, (2) suggested a new way to approach the homework, (3) suggested going back to the old approach if her new technique didn't have positive results, and (4) set a time limit. Her teacher will probably grant her request.

TEACHERS WHO GIVE INSUFFICIENT EXPLANATIONS

Tom looked confused. The teacher had just finished explaining how she wanted the class to tackle a group project. Tom moved his chair into a small group with six other students. The first thing everyone said was, "What are we supposed to be doing? I'm confused." Tom raised his hand. "Could you give us more of an explanation?" The teacher replied, "Do the best you can."

How Tom Sees the Problem

> Everyday I come to this class and I feel so stupid. A lot of the others feel the same way. How can we do our best if we don't know what's going on?

How the Teacher Sees It

> For the past three days I've been explaining how they should do their group projects. They need to try the project first and *then* ask me more questions.

How Not to Handle It

> *Tom:* Our group really has no idea what you want. Either answer these questions or provide us with a good example from a past project. We deserve that much.

Thumbs down! If Tom took this approach, he would probably not get Ms. Lynch to agree to either option. No one likes to hear ultimatums.

How to Handle It

Have the group write a list of clarification questions. Your goal is to get a clearer picture of what the teacher wants or expects. The teacher will be much more inclined to provide a more in-depth explanation once she sees, in writing, a detailed list of specific questions.

Ask the teacher to give examples. Rather than asking the teacher to repeat herself, ask her to provide specific examples. Some teachers have samples of past projects on file. Ask her to provide an example of a good project paper.

> *Tom:* Ms. Lynch, my group has the following questions. We were also thinking that an example from a past project might help us to do our best. Do you have a sample? Or can you answer these questions? We'd greatly appreciate either form of your help.

Tom gets an A+ for his efforts! He (1) stated what he wanted, and (2) provided options. People are much more likely to cooperate when they are given options.

TEACHERS WHO NEVER SEEM TO WANT TO HELP

Lisa, a college freshman, said:

> I have a basic writing course. I'm not a writer, so I had a few problems with the class. When I tried to talk to the professor after class, he said, "I have office hours, you know. Come see me then." But when I went to see him during office hours, he was either not there or busy on the telephone. Finally, when I did talk to him, he acted as if his mind was somewhere else, or he was in a hurry to go, he doesn't understand my problem.

How Lisa Sees the Problem

> Professors are not forced to teach us; it is a job they chose to pursue. They should want to help their students as much as possible.

How the Professor Sees It

Too many students have come to me over the years wanting my help, just so they can pass the course. They're not really turned on by the subject matter, and they're not really motivated. They just want to know what's on the test, or what they can do to get an A. It makes me feel manipulated. And I don't feel like helping under these circumstances.

How to Handle It

Your goal is to get the teacher to help you without him feeling used. Take time to talk to him at times when you don't need help. A teacher will feel flattered to know that you are taking a special interest in his subject matter. Many teachers feel that their subject is the most important. By asking questions and showing interest in other aspects of the class, the teacher will be more willing to listen when you need help.

Teachers Who are Boring and Robtic

What can you do about boring, robotic teachers? Brad had just finished his presentation to the class, reading a paper that took him the entire semester to compose. He enthusiastically described his theory, research, and results. Now he turned to his professor, hoping to get a smile, a look of approval, or some sign that his presentation was well done. "Even if he had flared his nostrils—that would have been helpful," Brad said. But the professor didn't even blink.

Brad had just encountered Dr. Robot. Busy with research and writing, Robots have no time or interest in engaging students intellectually or emotionally. Try visiting one of them during office hours and you'll get the same cold, clammy reaction. Typically, students feel they should start the conversation with an apology "Ah, I'm really sorry to bother you like this, but . . ."

How to Handle It

The secrets of coping with Robots are:

- Don't expect any kind of emotional reaction.

- Visit them only during scheduled office hours. Keep the visit short and businesslike.

- Be specific when discussing your ideas.
- Talk only about the subject at hand.
- Be prepared—have your questions or proposal ready and in writing.
- Thank them for their time, but don't expect any kind of acknowledgment.

SUMMARY

When dealing with apathetic teachers, find ways to take care of your own needs. Tact and diplomacy can help in getting them to be more responsive teachers. Also, be sure to have alternative ways to get the information you need.

3

Know-It-Alls: Dr. Encyclopedia and Dr. Charlatan

There are professors who claim they know it all and they really do. Then, there are the imposters—buffoons who pretend they know everything but know very little. How do you tell the difference?

Dr. Encyclopedia welcomes, for the most part, an opportunity to expound on his knowledge, while *Dr. Charlatan* is quick to judge, belittle, and dismember student ideas. Dr. Charlatan is suspicious of students who ask him questions; he assumes they're trying to "catch him" on something he doesn't know. Both Dr. Encyclopedia and Dr. Charlatan are difficult to deal with because they tend to be condescending and pompous. A college freshman said, "I dislike when a teacher has the attitude that 'the only reason I'm wasting my time being here is because they're paying me.'" A college sophomore said, "I don't like it when a professor takes on this haughty, superior attitude of 'I'm the professor; you're the student; therefore, I'm right.'"

Coping With Dr. Encyclopedia and Dr. Charlatan

Dealing with Dr. Encyclopedia is a bit easier than dealing with Dr. Charlatan. You can offer to perform some minor tasks for him, such as checking a book out of the library, making some photocopies, or performing some minor secretarial duty for him. In this way, you ingratiate yourself to him and lead him to believe that he is in the company of a promising scholar. He will therefore be more inclined to give you a B+ on the paper you concocted over the weekend, rather than the C- you deserve.

Talk to him after class and during office hours. Take notes on what he has to say. Later, when you tell him you can't make it to the exam at the scheduled time because you're sick, he'll be more inclined to believe you.

It's also a good idea to talk occasionally after class with Dr. Charlatan, but let him select the subject. Don't ask very many questions. He tends to view questions suspiciously. The best way to carry on an after-class discussion with Dr. Charlatan is simply to let him go on talking, without interruption, for as long as he wants to speak. Just stare at him, dumbfounded, as he speaks. When he finishes, say something like, "Wow! I'll really have to stop and think about that. It was really over my head!" If you get on the good side of Dr. Charlatan, he may agree to let you substitute a collage for a thirty page term paper. Then take your learning into your own hands and study your true interests.

TEACHERS WHO CRITICIZE YOUR IDEAS

Donna, a college sophomore, said, "I have an English teacher who enjoys feeling superior. He likes to go around the room soliciting everyone's opinions, but when he heard mine he said, out loud, in front of the entire class, "Out of everyone's, I believe yours is the most irrelevant and uninteresting."

How Donna Sees It

I wanted to punch this guy. He is pompous and arrogant.

How the Know-It-All Sees It

Some people are just not college material. They should go on to vocational colleges, not be enrolled in courses at top universities.

HOW NOT TO HANDLE IT

Donna: How dare you call my ideas "irrelevant and uninteresting!" You have no right to do that!

Know-it-alls do not back down and apologize. They simply use their status and power to make things worse. Donna could expect to receive a vendetta grade. Also, being a counter know-it-all is never effective.

Emotional harangues and threats can be seen as further "proof" by the arrogant teacher that Donna's work isn't up to par.

How to Handle It

Donna's best strategy is to confront the know-it-all after class and ask for more information.

> *Donna:* Dr. Smith, I would like more information. In class, you said that my opinions were "irrelevant and uninteresting." Could you explain that further?

Donna's tone of voice is particularly important in this transaction. She should sound genuinely interested in hearing more and should listen carefully once the professor begins to elaborate. She will learn how the teacher sees it. After the professor finishes, Donna can say, "You've given me a lot to think about. I'd like to write an essay stating my own point of view. Can we work this out for extra credit?"

By speaking up, Donna will have accomplished two things: (1) The know-it-all will have learned that he cannot use Donna as the class target because she confronts rather than seething silently. (2) By writing an essay, Donna will have a chance to show the know-it-all that her opinions are well thought out and intriguing. She also gains extra credit!

One last word. The professor was definitely out of line when he confronted Donna. She should begin documenting any future transactions both in and out of class with this arrogant instructor. If the verbal abuse continues, she can wage a formal complaint and he will be reprimanded. If its documented that he has insulted several students, this exposure will force him to come to terms with his behavior.

SUMMARY

1. Act professionally; be aware of tone of voice, body language, and appearance.

2. Avoid taking classes with arrogant know-it-all types, if at all possible.

3. If the know-it-all is the only professor who teaches the course, try to find out, in advance:

   (a) His grading policy

(b) The amount of work he expects

(c) His class attendance policy

4. Never confront a know-it-all in front of the entire class. Dr. Arthur R. Pell, who edited the updated version of Dale Carnegie's book *How to Win Friends and Influence People* (1982) says, "Try to have your visit in a place where your conversation will be private." The general rule of thumb: Praise people in public; confront them in private.

4

Nonlisteners: Ms. Illistenacy* and Mr. Inflexible

Some teachers refuse to listen or be flexible regardless of extenuating circumstances. *Ms. Illistenacy* and *Mr. Inflexible* will falsely accuse you, or single you out for punishment. They already have their minds made up before you have even had a chance to speak. Here's what you can do.

WHEN A TEACHER FALSELY ACCUSES YOU

Gina, a ninth grade high school student, said:

> I was taking a weekly test and I had a question about something. I went up to her desk and waited for her to finish what she was reading before I asked my question. When she looked up, she realized that she had left the answers to the test in plain view. She immediately accused me of cheating, even though I was the top student in the class, and she gave me a zero on the test.

How Gina Sees It

> She wouldn't listen. I tried to explain that I have a question, but she said, 'The answers were in plain view. I'm giving you an F.'

---

*Illistenacy: I first heard the word *illistenacy*, coined by professor Charles Swanson of Fairmont State College, at the 1991 International Listening Association Convention in Atlanta, Georgia. Swanson felt that since there was a term for the inability to read—*illiteracy*—there should also be a term that refers to the inability to listen, he coined the term *illistenacy*.

How the Teacher Sees It

Why did she stand there so long in silence? She must have been memorizing the answer sheet!

How Not to Handle It

Gina: How dare you accuse me of cheating! I am a straight A student in this class! I'm telling my parents about this!!

Gina will win the battle but lose the war. She should stick to her goal, a make-up exam—rather than focusing on the teacher's flaws, which will accomplish nothing.

How to Handle It

Suggest that the teacher give you a make-up test.

Gina: I'd like an opportunity to take a make-up exam, Ms. Wood.

Your goal is to have an opportunity to show the teacher that you know the material. Stick to getting your goal accomplished.

The Teacher Who Singles You Out For Undeserved Punishment

Mel, a high school sophomore, walked into her geometry class before the final bell rang. She approached a classmate and playfully pounded on his back with her fists. "Hey, Doug! Today's my birthday! Aren't you going to wish me a happy birthday!?"

The teacher looked up at that moment and saw Mel "punching" Doug. She sent her to see the dean.

How Mel Sees It

She wouldn't hear me out. She didn't want to hear my side.

How the Teacher Sees It

Melanie is very talkative. I made up my mind that the next time I caught her doing something, I was going to send her to the dean.

How Not to Handle It

Mel: Dean Jones, I didn't do anything!!!! She is so unfair! All I did was punch my friend on the back!!! We were just playing. That teacher is such a rude woman!

The dean will hear that Mel feels persecuted. He will also feel that Mel is calling the teacher names and will be less inclined to sympathize with her.

How to Handle It

Mel needs to explain to the dean in information mode exactly what happened. She should describe the incident as objectively as possible.

Mel: Dean Jones, today is my birthday! I went up to Doug and asked him if he was going to wish me a happy birthday. I playfully hit him on the back. The final bell hadn't rung yet. Doug will tell you the identical story.

Notice that Mel doesn't mention anything about the teacher. She sticks to the facts. Most likely, if she is a good student who stays out of trouble, she will not be penalized.

The Teacher Who Has Inflexible Rules

Frank, a high school senior, said,

Last year, I was on the golf team. School ends at 2:50 and the golf matches start at 3:30, so I had to be dismissed from my last period class early. The teacher didn't like this and started giving me a zero for participation and a zero for any quizzes I missed. Up until golf season started I was a straight A student in her class. I tried to talk to her but she just wouldn't listen or consider any other alternatives. It took my parents speaking to the principal, the principal speaking to me, and then the principal speaking to the teacher before the problem was resolved. Although the problem was finally resolved, I could tell the teacher didn't like me after that and it was reflected in my grade.

How Frank Sees It

This teacher is unfair and inflexible.

How the Inflexible Teacher Sees It

Golf should not take precedence over my class. My policies apply equally to all. If you miss a quiz for whatever reason, you get a zero. No make-ups. It's simple, straight-forward, and fair to all.

How to Handle It

Although Frank did get the matter resolved, his grade suffered. There is a better way. He could have had the golf coach approach his teacher.

Frank: Coach, my sixth period teacher has been giving me zeros for absenteeism and missed quizzes ever since golf season started. I'm willing to make up the quizzes, but she won't hear me out. Do you have any suggestions?

Teachers are more likely to help when they are asked for suggestions. Since the coach is on an equal par with the teacher, she'll be able to get her point across much more effectively than the dean or the principal, whose superior authority tends to overrule teachers.

Sometimes it does pay to talk to the dean, especially if an inflexible teacher sends you there. This is the way high school junior resolved a matter after he was sent to the dean by an inflexible teacher.

I had a bandana on and so did two girls. The teacher told me to take mine off. I said, "Well, what about them?" She replied, "They are girls." She said it was a part of their outfit. I disagreed. I said I'd take mine off if the girls would. She sent me to the dean. I came back to class . . . with my bandana on.

SUMMARY

1. *Hear them out, even if they don't hear you out.* At least you'll know where they're coming from. You'll be able to tell their side of the story—and yours—to the dean or the principal. Higher authorities will be more inclined to believe you if you present both points of view in an unimpassioned manner.

2. *Don't expect them to start listening.* Some teachers are locked into their own inflexible opinions and nothing is going to change their mind. Stick to the facts when you talk to them. Instead of changing their perceptions, get them to agree to trying something new.

3. *Document for self-protection.* Write down your side of the story. Tell higher authorities that the teacher wouldn't listen to your point of view. Back up your side of the story with a lot of facts. Remember to present your case in information mode.

5

Vendetta Graders

Some teachers are known to have biased grading systems. They often have pets and award higher grades to those they favor. Some lower the grades of students who disagree with them. These are known as *Vendetta Graders*. This kind of teacher is not always easy to detect at first, as in the case of *Dr. Nice.*

THE NOT-SO-NICE POTENTIAL OF DR. NICE

Ask any student what course to take to get an *easy A* and they'll tell you, "Oh, take a course with Dr. Nice! He's so nice and easy!" Dr. Nice *rarely gives tests*. His classes are generally a *friendly rap session* in which he describes his trip to India, his guru, and his Japanese gardens. Dr. Nice's main purpose is to make sure that everybody likes him, which is exactly why Dr. Nice is potentially a very difficult person.

A college freshman described an incident with a "nice" teacher.

> I had an English teacher who was very active in the women's movement. Everybody said she was so nice—easy to get an A, lots of in-class discussions on exciting topics, and essay papers where you write about your personal feelings on things. We had to write four very controversial papers throughout the semester on such topics as abortion, sex discrimination, etc. She was very much for abortion and I am very much against it. I said so in my first paper and I got a C-. The next three papers (two on sex discrimination and the other I can't remember), my opinions just happened to agree with hers (coincidentally, not on purpose) and I got three A's. Maybe, just maybe, the quality of the writing on my first paper was horrible and the other three were great, but I

doubt it. The point is that she didn't grade me on my writing ability but instead on my opinions. I ended up getting a B+ in her class, so I can't really complain, but other students weren't so lucky—like the guys. It seems that this teacher was nice so long as you agreed with her opinion on things. If you didn't, your grade was lowered.

Here's another example of what a "nice" teacher might do:

In high school, I had a teacher who did not like northerners, which I am. I was not getting very good grades in her class. Then, one day, I mentioned after class that my grandfather was originally from Mississippi. After that, I started getting very good grades in her class. Everybody told me that this teacher was very nice. Since I was the only northerner in the class, I didn't get to see the nice side of this "nice" teacher until I talked about my grandfather. It seems that getting a good grade from her had a price.

How to Handle Vendetta Graders

There are two ways to handle teachers who have biased grading systems: (1) Find out what pleases them and live up to their expectations. (2) Document what happens to you and wage a formal complaint with the dean or a grades appeal committee.

Choosing the latter course, however, does not guarantee positive results. You may discover that the dean is best friends with the teacher. Members of a grades appeal committee may also be friends with the professor. People who work together are inclined to side with their colleagues.

This isn't to suggest that you should not appeal to higher authorities, but you're more likely to get positive results if the complaint is brought about by several students. There is power in numbers. Before you proceed, weigh the consequences. If you decide to document and wage a formal complaint, ask yourself first:

- What will happen if the dean doesn't take my complaint seriously?

- Will I be better or worse off?

If you decide it's not worth the risk you can either:

- Study the behavior of the successful students who are getting good grades from this teacher. Ask yourself, What do they do? Do they smile a lot? Do they pay her compliments? Do they sit up front and look interested in learning? Do they volunteer? Do they help after class? Observe successful students and see if there's something positive they're doing. If it works, you might want to try it. Remember, your goal is to get a good grade. If positive, enthusiastic behavior helps you reach your goal, why not go for it?

- Switch to another class.

Sometimes appealing works and sometimes it doesn't. Here are three true life stories. Two of the students appealed and it worked. One did not get positive results. Read each story and ask yourself: Why did appealing work for the first two students but not for the last? Under what circumstances would I want to appeal? Under what circumstances might I opt to try changing my own behavior and attitudes instead?

APPEALS WITH POSITIVE RESULTS

Student 1

I had a professor for a cognitive psychology course who announced the first day of class, "Most of you will flunk this course. It is very difficult. If you don't plan to work hard, you might as well drop out right now." Most of us thought this was just an empty threat, so we stayed.

After the first exam, however, several of us changed our minds. On his multiple choice test we were asked the pettiest and most trivial things—information that was not covered during class. Some of the information was embedded in footnotes and sidebars of our textbook. Several of us decided to see the dean. We took our exams and the textbook along as evidence. The dean promised to confront the professor. Obviously, he kept his promise because we saw a real difference.

First, the professor announced he would drop our lowest test score from our final grade. Next, he started providing us with summary sheets concerning what would be emphasized on the test. Everyone felt so much better and most of us ended up passing the course with an A or B.

Incidentally, I think our talking to the dean was a real turning point for this cranky professor. Overweight and sloppily dressed, he shortly thereafter went on a very strict diet and running regimen. Several years later I saw him in a health food restaurant and barely recognized him. A friend of mine said, "Do you know who that is?" He looked like a completely different person. His attitude seemed very different, too. He even nodded at us and smiled.

Student 2

I was given a schedule change into another class because of an unpredicted overflow of seniors this year. There wasn't enough room in English for all of them. I decided to give the new teacher a chance because it was only fair. After the first week in her class, I was so frustrated, I could barely think. This teacher picked favorites in class and was very public about it. I knew that I was never going to learn anything in there because of the way she taught. I approached her and told her my problem and she just brushed me off, like it was my fault. She wouldn't talk to me after that.

I went through the system to get a schedule change. I started with my counselor, then went to the coordinator of curriculum, and finally to our principal. I really believe going through the system will work for the individual.

An Appeal with Negative Results

In graduate school I took an upper level course that was team taught by two adjunct professors. The course was trite and I showed my displeasure by rolling my eyes and smirking when the professors would make us break into small groups to play ridiculous touchy-feely games.

The two professors held me after class one day and asked me what I thought about their course. I told them it was the most stupid and ridiculous class I had ever taken in my whole entire life. "Several of the other students feel the same way," I informed them.

After that, it seemed that everything I did in that class was wrong. They would call on me and criticize all of my answers. I started to brace myself for a vendetta grade. I began documenting all my conversations with them. When I received a failing grade in this class, I took all my documentation to the dean. The dean set up a grades appeal committee.

At the meeting, the professors were given all the time in the world to explain and justify why they had given me a failing grade. I, on the other hand, was given five minutes to speak. The committee said they would notify me by mail. The grade stayed as is. I ended up transferring to another university, which meant that I lost several credits in the process.

SUMMARY

You feel that the grade you were issued is unfair. What can you do?

1. Find out what *does* please the teacher and live up to their expectations. Perhaps the teacher gives a lot of weight to students who participate in class. If that's the case, then start raising your hand and participating more often. Sure, you might feel a little shy at first, but with practice you may even begin to enjoy speaking up. Also, the more involved you become, the more you will remember and retain, which is bound to raise your grade.

But what happens if you feel you have done everything to live up to the teacher's expectations and you *still* received an undeserved low grade? The first thing you should do is hold a conference with the teacher. Bring all your papers, homework, quizzes, test scores, essays, and anything else that your grade was based upon. Go over it with the teacher. Some teachers are willing to change the marks if its an honest mistake on their part. If after the conference you feel that the grade is undeserved, make an appointment to speak with the principal, the chairperson, or someone else who is higher up, such as a dean. The person who supervises your teacher will listen to you and help you get positive results. Make sure, however, that you explain your side very logically. Lay out all the papers; show the syllabus. Explain very clearly why you feel your grade should be higher *without* making a personal attack or character assassination on the teacher.

2. Document what happens to you and wage a formal complaint. Any time you take time to document (that is, keep a log of any and all transactions you've had with the teacher), people *know* that you mean serious business. List the facts and the dates. Sometimes the only way to deal with aggressive, nasty people is to let them know that you are going to take any measures available to you to have justice rendered. Here's a sample of what you might say in a letter:

Example: On (state the date), I submitted the first report that was due in (state the class, subject, etc.).

3. List the behavior that you feel was prejudiced against you and resulted in a vendetta grade.

Example: When I turned in the report, you said, "Anyone who had to be corrected for wearing a hat in my class probably doesn't do a very good report."

4. List additional facts and dates.

Example: On (state the date), I met with you to review all of the essays I have written during the semester and compare them to the criteria set forth on your syllabus.

5. List additional comments that indicate prejudice.

Example: You commented, "I don't have the time to re-read these. If your attitude had improved, you probably would have done better."

6. State that you intend to take any measures available to you to resolve the issue.

6

Beware of the Crazy-making Double Binders

I've adopted this term from Herb Goldberg and George Bach, authors of the classic *Creative Aggression* (1974). A *Crazy-making Double Binder* (CMDB) is someone who literally makes you feel like you're being bounced off walls. Ask a CMDB what you should do for your class project and he'll say, "Oh, use your imagination. Whatever interests you is fine with me." Six weeks later, you give him a progress report and he snaps, "I find this project totally unacceptable. You'll have to start all over again." Every time class meets, Professor CMDB throws out a different set of *hints* concerning what it takes to get a good grade in the course. But no one seems to know exactly what he wants. Pretty soon, everyone starts feeling crazy.

A CMDB is usually a very moody person—up and enthusiastic one day, down in the dumps and angry the next; pleased that you ask him a question after class one day, irritated the next. His policies are inconsistent and unclear to students. Here's how high school and college students described CMDB teachers:

- He is usually careless about deadlines, changing his mind frequently.

- It is impossible to discover what he wants.

- He says one thing and does another.

- He says we need to know the textbook, and then he contradicts the text on his multiple choice tests and marks our answers wrong. When you confront him, he says, "You should have listened to me instead."

- He makes whimsical on-the-spot changes to the syllabus.

- My teacher took the first 10 minutes of class talking to a student from another class; then she turned around and yelled at the class and took off points for talking.

- I had a teacher who was lenient one day and strict the next. One day he said 93.2 is an A; then the next day he said 93.7 is a B+.

- With some teachers you don't know if it's one of those days when you can play around with them. Or, is it one of those days when they might write you up for playing around with them.

Vague and Inconsistent Policies

The following are four true-life stories that college students shared with me about being involved with professors who were CMDBs:

A certain teacher required his pupils to purchase a book he had written. During the semester, the book was barely, if ever, mentioned. Almost all lecture material and assignments came from the regular textbook. When the final was given, hardly anything from the lectures or textbook was on it—it consisted almost entirely of the material from his book! On top of that, the bookstores refused to buy back the book!

During the writing of my thesis my advisor trashed 70 pages of work because he disagreed with one of my points, even though it was a supported theory. I rewrote it all, not wanting to fail. He then told me I had only shown minimum improvement because "I couldn't do better." I proceeded to do what he wanted and even more. Then he evaluated my final paper and graded me low because in the new version I hadn't included the material which was in the the first 70 pages he had trashed!

I turned in a project which was a drawing. The teacher stated that certain lines did not have to be in the drawing. So, I took out the excess lines. The professor then asked his teaching assistant to grade the final drawing. He took off points for the lines the teacher told me to remove!

My history teacher started yelling at the class and freaking out regarding all the work he had to do and how the final grades were due and how he had a report to do for someone and all this stuff. Then he told us to hand in a whole bunch of work, but he complained about how he's going to have to grade it all. Then, with all this commotion, he lost seven students' quizzes. If it were one or two, I'd say it was the students' fault, but seven! Then he wouldn't let them retake the test because he didn't want to grade any more papers!

How to Handle It

1. Ask for clarification. Ask the teacher to objectively describe any vague term he may use. When he talks about "good" students who get the good grades, ask him, "What exactly do you mean by 'good?' " Find out *exactly* what he wants.

When he says, "You can turn in your projects *later on* in the semester," find out exactly when "later on" is supposed to be. In one class, "later on" turned out to be the following day!

2. Insist that the teacher put his criteria for passing the course in writing. Tell him that you (the class) want a syllabus that spells out the specifics for getting an A, B, C, etc.

3. Present an outline of your plans. Have the teacher initial it so he can't say, six weeks from now, that he never approved your project.

4. Level with the CMDB in a non-threatening way. Often, there is very little relationship between what a CMDB covers in class and what is on his tests. To help determine what might be on his tests, you should:

a. Talk with him after class or during office hours. Tell him you enjoy his class very much and that you would like to do well on the upcoming exam. If he replies, "Well, then study everything!" tell him, "I have studied everything, but I think that the heart of the matter lies in chapter 7. Do you agree?"

b. Talk to former students to get a feel for the kinds of things that might appear on his tests. Find out if there are any old tests available.

c. Read what he's published. This will give you a good idea of what interests him most and will probably be a good clue about what he emphasizes on a test.

d. Analyze the test to see if you can discover the kinds of information he emphasized, if you do poorly on the midterm. Many students who use this approach perform significantly better on the final exam.

SUMMARY

Some teachers clearly communicate what they expect from their students, while other teachers present only a vague picture of what they want. It's easy to proceed on an assignment when the expectations are spelled out up front, but how does one deal with a Crazy-making Double Binder who tells you what they want one day, then criticizes you the next day for following their instructions?! Here's what to do:

1. Make sure the grading guidelines are clearly spelled out before you begin your assignment. If the teacher hasn't published his criteria for evaluation in a syllabus, then you need to *ask* him what he wants and expects.

2. Take notes when he explains what he thinks he's looking for. Ask a lot of questions. Whenever he says something vague, like, "Well, I expect you to use your imagination," tell him that you'll get back to him with a one hundred word statement describing what your imagination has come up with. Make sure you get him to initial the statement before you proceed on the big project.

3. Keep checking back. If you've spotted any of the warning signals that let you know you're dealing with a CMDB (giving vague messages, changing his mind, criticizing you for following his directions, etc.), then it's an absolute *must* that you continue to communicate with (and document) this teacher on a frequent basis as you proceed with your project.

7

Teachers Who Criticize and Embarrass Students In Front of Peers

A high school senior wrote,

> During the SAT review, many of the teachers were under extreme pressure because of deadlines. They became irritable and unreasonable—at least that's what students thought. One teacher became completely unreasonable and crossed the line from irritable to insulting. After criticizing the entire class, he singled me out and tore me down for not having a certain handout. Then he yelled at me for my posture! He said I always lean against the wall. At the moment, I wasn't resting against the wall and I told him so, so he said, "Yes, but look how you're leaning on your elbows." I just tried to remain calm but I felt I was being persecuted for no good reason. He's just a very critical teacher who likes to embarrass students in front of peers."

Sound familiar? They purposely call on you when they know you don't have the answer, just to embarrass you. They write overly critical comments on papers. You ask a question and feel about two inches high when the teacher responds, "I already covered that. Where were you?" Isn't there anything positive they can say? In this chapter we'll examine strategies for dealing with five types of critical teachers:

- The critical name caller
- The indirect insulter
- The sadist

- The verbal abuser
- The nitpicker

THE CRITICAL NAME CALLER

Howard, a high school freshman, said,

> I didn't finish my work and the teacher told me to stay after school to finish it. She said I was a stupid moron.

How Howard Sees It

> This teacher is trying to make me feel inferior. She obviously doesn't like me.

How the Teacher Sees It

> Howard is always goofing off just to get attention.

HOW NOT TO HANDLE IT

> *Howard:* Ms. Blalock, I understand that you want me to complete my work and you have every right to criticize me for not doing so. But you do not have the right to mortify me in front of the entire class. If you ever do that again, I plan to tell the principal, the dean, and my parents.

Howard has the right to confront and threaten the teacher, but it is not the most effective action. Threats rarely make a situation better. When people have been threatened, their natural inclination is to retaliate.

HOW TO HANDLE IT

A teacher has the right to request that you stay after school to complete your work. She does not have the right, however, to call you names. About half of the 200 students I interviewed for this book reported incidents where difficult teachers verbally abused them. This behavior from a teacher cannot ever be justified, no matter what the student has said or done. It is abuse. If I were the principal I would severely reprimand a teacher who verbally abuses a student. Unfortunately, we live in a world filled with imperfect bureaucracies where fairness does not always reign. Some principals side with their teachers and trivialize students' complaints.

Howard has to work a very long school year with this difficult teacher.

His first strategy, therefore, is to diplomatically approach her after school and use expert communication skills. The goal is to get her to stop calling him names without alienating her.

> *Howard*: Ms. Blalock, when you called me a "stupid moron" I felt absolutely mortified. I realize I was wrong for not completing my work on time, but I would appreciate if you showed your concern for me without calling me names. I enjoy your class and I will try my best to get my work completed on time from now on.

Howard did a great job! He:

- described the offending behavior objectively,

- told the teacher how he felt,

- explained that he understood her concern for his uncompleted work,

- told what he expected from the teacher in the future,

- paid the teacher a sincere compliment, and

- told her what he plans to do in the future.

The teacher was gently reprimanded in a way that should curtail any future verbal attacks. In the future, Howard should keep a record of any transactions with this teacher. If the teacher calls Howard a derrogatory name a second time, he and his parents should speak to the principal. Verbal abuse is a serious offense.

THE INDIRECT INSULTER

John, an eighth grader, said,

> There are only eleven students in my advanced algebra class. I've been having a really bad year and can't keep up with the class. One day I failed another test. The teacher said that anyone who failed the test was an idiot. I was the only one who failed it. I got upset and left. The class got mad at the teacher and everyone started yelling.

How John Sees It

I was already feeling bad. His comment made me furious.

How the Teacher Sees It

> That test was so easy. These are advanced students, the cream of the crop. If a student fails one of these tests, he's not applying

himself. John is bright. Maybe if I say something in front of the whole class, it will motivate him to do better.

How Not to Handle It

In the original transaction, John chose to walk out of the classroom, and the class started yelling at the teacher. The only thing this accomplished was hurt feelings and resentment. People have to sit down and talk with each other to get things resolved. This is how all conflict comes to a positive resolution.

How to Handle It

John should wait until after class to confront the teacher. Since he's not doing well, he may want to discuss more than the teacher's immediate, indirect, insulting comments.

> *John:* Mr. Brody, I realize that I am the only one who failed the test, so when you said, "Anyone who failed that test is an idiot," I felt really upset. I didn't appreciate that comment, but I'd also like to discuss other options. I'm thinking of switching to another class . . .

The teacher's comment is used as a catalyst for a much needed discussion. John should explore options with the teacher, while at the same time, making it clear that he wants to be treated with respect if he stays. He may use the conference time as an opportunity to explain why he's doing so poorly (sickness, family problems, etc.)

The Sadist

Russ, a college sophomore, wrote,

> A certain art history teacher (I shall name no names) gave ten question quizzes every Friday. One time I overslept and woke up five minutes before class. Rushing to class (I got there five minutes late), I found the door was locked tight. I knocked on the door several times, and even banged on it, but he didn't open the door until 10 minutes later, when he announced with this amused smirk on his face, "You missed the quiz."

> That really ticked me off, but what was I supposed to say? I was late, and I did know it was a quiz day. But you'd think he'd have some compassion and let someone in who's only five minutes

late and banging on the door. (It was my first time being late, too. It's not like I do this all the time.) And then to have the nerve to open up the door when the quiz is over and act like he had no idea I was there! To me, that shows the height of contempt for both me and for other students in general. And this wasn't an isolated incident.

What could I have done? I should have grabbed him by the scruff of his neck, tied him to the back of my ten-speed, and dragged him through the streets (probably to the cheers of thousands of students!—Just kidding.)

How the Teacher Sees It

It really infuriates me when students walk in late, especially in the middle of a quiz. Don't they realize how disruptive that is for the other students? What if I allowed everyone to just walk in during a quiz whenever they feel like it? There'd be chaos!!!

I need to teach him a lesson. He thinks he can come to class late and still take the quiz? I'll show him. I'll use him as an example. That way no one will be late in the future.

How Not to Handle It

Russ: you really made me feel embarrassed when you made me wait outside while the rest of the class was taking the quiz. You could see I was banging on the door! Sure, I was late, but it's the first time!

This doesn't work because it doesn't help Russ to get what he wants: an opportunity to make up the quiz. Criticizing the teacher will not help him achieve his goal.

How to Handle It

Russ needs to find out the professor's policies. If the professor already announced at the beginning of the semester, "My policy is to lock the door promptly after the bell rings. So, if you are late for class, you won't be able to get in until after the quiz," then Russ has no basis for any kind of complaint. However, if the professor did not announce his policy up front, then Russ certainly needs to confront him.

Russ: Dr. Brane, I was five minutes late for class today and I apologize for that. It is not like me. What is your policy on tardiness? If it is permissable, I'd like to take the quiz now?

If Dr. Brane announces that his policy is no make up on missed quizzes, Russ can gently ask, "Since it's not like me to be late, I'm wondering if you'd make an exception to the rule. I realize I was out of line for being late, and I apologize. Would you consider reneging your policy this one time?"

By talking in information mode, and repeating what he wants, Russ may succeed in getting Dr. Brane to reconsider, especially since Russ' second request was accompanied by a second apology.

THE VERBAL ABUSER

Vana, a ninth grader, said,

I have a teacher who gives lectures the whole period. Then he tests us once a week and his tests have nothing to do with his lectures. So one day, I said out loud, 'I haven't learned anything,' and he told me, 'If you were smarter than what you are, you would open a book for once in your life.' That really made me mad.

How Vana Sees It

I don't like it when a teacher embarrasses me in front of the whole class. This teacher needs to learn how to teach!

How the Teacher Sees It

When a student embarrasses me in front of the whole class, I have no choice but to give a retort. I can't let a student get away with that kind of behavior.

HOW NOT TO HANDLE IT

Vana: I haven't learned anything and neither have the others. You need to learn how to teach!

The teacher won't know what Vana is really complaining about. Is it his teaching style? Is it the content of the quizzes? Does he spend too much time lecturing? If Vana can tell Mr. Moro, in information mode, what the problem is, he and she will be able to reach a resolution. Perhaps Mr. Moro will design other ways to present the material besides lecture. Or perhaps Vana will learn how to skim the textbook to prepare for the quizzes.

How to Handle It

Vana needs to wait until after class to express her opinions about the class. Otherwise, she is setting herself up for a counterattack from a difficult teacher. (A non-difficult teacher would speak to her after class about her inappropriate comment. He might begin with a question, "Tell me what prompted your remark, Vana?" and might even learn something useful.)

Vana: Mr. Moro, I am having problems with this class.

Vana can then objectively describe the discrepancy between Mr. Moro's lectures and the contents of his quizzes.

The Nitpicker

James, a tenth grader, said,

She said she didn't like my hair. I told her I didn't come to school to please her. I came to learn. Then she wrote me up and sent me to the dean's office. That really made me mad.

How James Sees It

She has no right to criticize my hair. This is a free country! Then when I told her this, she got me in more trouble. The dean called my grandmother. I feel so mad.

How the Teacher Sees It

James has a wild hair-do to purposely get attention from the rest of the class. He is a distraction. Someone needs to confront him. He's going to have a hard time getting a job with that kind of hair-do. And he should not talk back to teachers! I'm teaching him a lesson!

How Not to Handle It

James: Who do you think you're talking to? I don't come to school to please you! I don't know where you're getting off on that stuff! This is a free country and I'll wear my hair any way I please!!!

The teacher will feel defensive and will be more inclined to use her authority and power to put a lid on this conversation.

How to Handle It

James: You are entitled to your opinions, Ms. Harvey.

Tripple bravos for James!!! There's little a teacher can do about a student's personal choice of a hair style. Just tell her she has the right to her own opinions, smile, and walk away!

SUMMARY

Don't just let it fester when a difficult teacher criticizes you in front of your peers. He or she needs to be confronted. At first, try to deflect criticism without alienating the teacher by speaking in information mode. If the abuse continues, contact higher authorities. If the entire class is being constantly belittled and attacked, bring forth a group complaint and demand results.

8

A Deadly Trio–Dr. Explosion, Dr. Doomsday and Dr. Victim

How do you react when someone yells at you? About twenty percent of us get furious and scream back. Others withdraw into silence or sweeten their way out of conflict. But the vast majority of people feel confused, frightened, panicky, child-like, or paralyzed. They say and do nothing.

What about teachers who shoot down your ideas? A professor wrote across a students' project report for a business, "It'll never work." Good thing the student didn't listen to *Dr. Doomsday*. His idea was the foundation for Federal Express!

Some professors walk around as though they're carrying a cup of human blood that's been extracted by all the villians of the world who have done them dirty. They carry a long list of misdeeds committed against them by ex-wives, faculty members, and administrators.

Any student who's willing to listen will have an opportunity to hear their sorrowful, long-winded tales of woe. In this chapter, you'll learn what you can do to cope with the deadly trio of *Dr. Explosion, Dr. Doomsday* and *Dr. Victim*.

DR. EXPLOSION

How do you react when a professor suddenly explodes at you? Most students aren't quite sure what to do. The typical reaction is a frozen stance.

Mark raised his hand during the middle of the professor's lecture to ask a clarification question. The professor, suddenly volatile, yelled, "I am so sick and tired of having to come in here and teach a bunch of dull, idiotic, pea-brained, mentally deficient, dense imbeciles like you! I've had it!" And with that he kicked the waste can and stormed out of the room. The class was stunned.

How to Handle It

1. Don't yell back. If a professor screams at you, stand there and take it. Give him a "nothing look", an expressionless look that depicts absolutely no emotion. Appear disinterested.

2. Let his anger run its course. He'll eventually run out of steam, as long as you don't interject any comments.

3. Don't let your gaps in knowledge be obvious. Phrase questions so they appear to be sidebars to your already vast knowledge. In this way, Dr. Explosion will feel respect for you and he'll be less likely to make you the victim of his next temper tantrum.

Dr. Doomsday

There's nothing more potentially depressing than taking a class with Dr. Doomsday. Don't share your vision of world peace or your dreams of patenting the first inkless pen. Don't ever think of telling him you'd like to be a freelance writer or, worse yet, a movie star. Dr. Doomsday will be quick to tell you how shallow and unrealistic your goals are. He, too, wanted to do something "unrealistic" at one time. And it didn't work for him. So, it certainly won't work for a "twit" like you. Doomsdayers spend classtime discussing their morbid views of society, the world, and their dislike for today's unvirtuous, banal, ignorant, uncultured students.

The main secret for coping with Dr. Doomsday is to work on projects with other students, so you can keep your sanity and your sanguine perspectives on life.

Balance is the other key. You cannot handle, psychologically, more than one Dr. Doomsday per semester. If the course is required and taught only by Dr. Doomsday, make sure the other courses you take that semester are with upbeat or neutral professors. Talk with other students who have already had the classes you're planning to take. They'll help you avoid the academic doomsdayers.

DR. VICTIM

Closely alligned to the doomsdayers of academia are the Dr. Victims. But instead of focusing their negativity on the world, their sole topic of interest is themselves. Imagine entering a professor's office and he starts complaining about his colleagues, his workload, and Mary, his ex-wife. What can you do?

Carefully interrupting, you might begin by saying, "I sympathize with your problems, sir. You sound very upset. This obviously is not a good time to discuss my paper with you. Can we reschedule this appointment for tomorrow?"

There's a good chance that Dr. Victim will suddenly snap out of his melodramatic mood and get down to business.

SUMMARY

Not all college professors are like the trio described in this chapter. There are many who are helpful, courteous, and genuinely concerned with the intellectual development of their students. Unfortunately, not everyone in academia can be described as charismatic, concerned, and inspiring. Futhermore, some of these negative character traits might be temporary as professors/instructors are only human and may let professional standards slip during bad times.

Always talk to your classmates. Form a network. They can help you keep your chin up when dealing with Dr. Doomsday, Dr. Explosion, or even Dr. Victim. Remember that individually, students can use coping strategies to get themselves through a rough situation, but collectively, students have increased power to affect change. However, avoid getting stuck in the divisionsal mindset of *Us vs. Them*. If the mutual goal is education, professors need students as much as students need professors. Conflict resolution begins when both sides recognize the need for the other.

9

Slave Drivers

Here it is again. Friday night. Your friends just called. "Hey! Come on over! You're missing a great party!"

"I can't," you reply. "Got a project that's going to take up my entire weekend. I've got to get started tonight."

"Again!?" says your friend. "You said that last weekend. And the weekend before. And the weekend before that!"

Every night, including weekends, while other people are kicking back, socializing or watching their favorite TV shows, you're studying. You're doing homework for a *Slave Driver*! Here's how students described this type of difficult teacher:

"She thinks her class is the *only* class."

"Doesn't he realize we have homework in all our other subjects, too?"

"Why does she always think her class is the most important?"

"It's just *too* much. And if you try to tell her, she just screams and embarrasses you in front of the entire class."

This is the profile of the dedicated, over-zealous teacher. She doesn't mind staying up until midnight grading a huge stack of papers. It's her duty. She wishes all teachers were as dedicated as she is.

How to Handle It

There are two basic strategies for handling the teacher who overworks you.

- The class can petition her.
- Examine your perception of the problem.

The Class Petition

It is strongly suggested that you approach the teacher who assigns too much work as part of the group. Otherwise, your complaints will most likely fall upon defensive ears. "All the other students are doing the work without complaining!" she'll snap. "You're just a cry baby!" The group, however, can petition the teacher. And if that doesn't work, they can take their complaints to the principal or other authority figures. Make sure that the evidence supporting the class opinions is well documented. Without this proof, it is unlikely that the class will succeed in getting the teacher to lighten the load.

Examine Your Perception of the Problem.

Sometimes it's not the work that's the problem but the student's perception of the work. Students who moan and groan and take three hours to complete a ten minute assignment are doing so for one of the following four reasons.

1. The student lacks the prerequisite course work necessary to easily complete the present assignment. Suggestions: Read lower level textbooks, hire a tutor, take an easier class.

2. The student is disorganized and has not developed efficient study habits and time management skills.

3. The student is experiencing emotional problems that get in the way of concentration (or his ability to concentrate).

4. The student is uncommitted. Without a firm commitment, students tend to dawdle, complain, oversleep, or watch too much T.V.

SUGGESTIONS FOR COPING

Increase Your Knowledge Base

Ask the teacher for books of a less difficult nature on the same topic. You can also hire a tutor, consult encyclopedias and/or other reference books, or repeat lower-level classes. Although it is initially very time-consuming to increase one's knowledge base, the end result is that work is completed more quickly and efficiently.

Get Organized

On Friday, Andy sat at his computer terminal with all his note cards and reference books in front of him, ready to begin his weekend project—a term paper. He sighed, stared at the keyboard, and twiddled his thumbs. Looking around his room, he noticed how disorganized it was. Soon, he was neatly stacking papers and folding laundry. In the process of straightening his room, he became acutely interested in a picture hanging lop-sided on his wall. He tried to straighten it, but it resumed its crooked position. Taking the picture down from the wall, he keenly noticed how much lighter the color of the wall was in that one spot.

By Saturday afternoon, Andy was busy painting the wall. By Sunday, he had decided to repaint the entire room. His desk, pushed to the middle of the room, was covered with a drop sheet. Underneath, his note cards and reference books lay, untouched.

Students can get way off track when they are not organized. Here are five ways to stop procrastinating.

1. *Use the "Swiss Cheese Approach"—i.e. take a stab at it.* Ever notice how a piece of Swiss cheese looks like someone took a pencil and stabbed it repeatedly? Imagine that your project is like that piece of Swiss cheese. Your goal is to put one hole in it, for a start. It's a good way to break the bad habit of procrastinating.

Begin anywhere on your project. By getting yourself in motion, you are more likely to stay in motion. Sometimes, all it takes is writing that first sentence, and then you're on your way.

2. *Set a time limit.* Another approach for ending procrastination is to set a time limit. Tell yourself, "I'll work on this project for only the next ten minutes." A short time commitment tends to make you feel less overwhelmed.

3. *"Everything in its place. A place for everything."* Have a specific place where you keep your books, papers, file cards, pens, pencils, erasers, etc. File folders are a must. That way, when you're ready to begin, everything will be at your fingertips and you won't waste any time searching for things.

4. *"I have nothing better to do."* Another approach is to unplug all telephones, turn off the television and radio, and chain up the refrigerator! Lock yourself in your room and say to yourself, "I really have nothing better to do right now, so I might as well work on this project."

5. *Get an early start.* It also pays to get started early on an assignment. You're less likely to feel the panic that brings on procrastination if you work systematically on a project from the first day.

DEAL WITH YOUR PROBLEMS, WORRIES, OR UNRESOLVED ANGER

Albert was not doing well in any of his classes, although he used to be a straight A student. His parents expected him to get good grades because they had serious plans to send him to an expensive college. They wanted to guarantee that their son would become a financial success. They hired an expensive, private tutor to come to their home six nights a week and assist Albert with all of his subjects. "Make sure he completes his homework in all of his courses," they insisted.

When Albert was reading his history textbook to the tutor, his voice sounded like a radio announcer. He frequently got off track and cracked jokes or wanted to tell the tutor about his social life. Finally, the tutor leveled with Albert. "Hey, what's going on with you? Seems to me you're not really interested in school."

Albert began to sob. He was not keen on his parents' plans for his future. He felt pressured and intimidated. He felt that anything less than an A in every subject was a sign of failure. He wanted to be accepted and loved even if he didn't become a high-powered executive, attorney, doctor, or CEO.

The tutor arranged for Albert and his parents to have an honest talk. The parents agreed to allow Albert to make more of his own decisions concerning his future. Albert came to realize that they were very concerned about him. He stopped procrastinating and started taking an interest in his school work again.

Students often procrastinate when they're feeling angry, confused, sad, or fearful. Talking helps. Some students confide in a close friend. Others talk to their parents, the school counselor, or a clergy member. Some students talk to themselves, in the form of a journal. They write down what's bothering them. By identifying the problem, they are more likely to come up with solutions. Once people talk out their problems, they are better able to concentrate, rather than procrastinate.

Make the Commitment

What is a commitment? How does a student know when he's truly committed to getting his school projects completed?

Committed students have goals. Perhaps the end goal is to become an engineer. Each class they take moves them closer to their goal. They realize that to be a top-of-the-line engineer requires many skills. They view all their projects as steps to help them become increasingly competent to reach their goal.

A committed student therefore gets the most out of his education. A committed student says to himself, "I will do whatever it takes to reach my goal."

Once a student is truly committed, it is much easier for him to begin and complete assignments—even from teachers who assign too much work.

SUMMARY

At times, teachers can be over-zealous about their subject matter. There are two basic strategies for coping with teachers who assign too much work:

1. The Class Petition is a way of showing unity as a group. Petitioning the teacher alone can be ineffective.

2. Examine your role in the problem:

• Am I a proscrastinator?

• Am I disorganized?

• Are there any emotional problems affecting my academic life?

• Do I lack some basic understanding of the information?

PART II

Higher Education: Pros and Cons

10

The Hazards of Graduate School

I was aware of what had reduced me to this *Student Prince Maudlin* state of mind. All the same, I couldn't help it. I had just spent five years in graduate school, a statement that may mean nothing to people who never served such a stretch; it is the explanation, nonetheless. I'm not sure I can give you the remotest idea of what graduate school is like. Nobody ever has. Millions of Americans now go to graduate school, but just say the phrase—"graduate school"—and what picture leaps into the brain? No picture, not even a blur. Half the people I knew in graduate school were going to write a novel about it. I thought about it myself. No one ever wrote such a book, as far as I know. Everyone used to sniff the air. How morbid! How poisonous! Nothing else like it in the world! But the subject always defeated them. It defied literary exploitation. Such a novel would be a study of frustration, but a form of frustration so exquisite, so ineffable, nobody could describe it. Try to imagine the worst part of the worst Antonioni movie you ever saw, or reading Mr. Sammler's "Planet" at one sitting, or just reading it, or being locked inside a Seaboard Railroad roomette, sixteen miles from Gainesville, Florida, heading north on the Miami-to-New York run, with no water and the radiator turning red in an amok psychotic overboil, and George McGovern sitting beside you telling you his philosophy of government. That will give you the general atmosphere.

—Tom Wolfe (1973)

Nineteen years after attempting to obtain a doctorate degree in mathematics at Stanford, Theodore Streleski walked into his professor's office and bludgeoned him to death with a two pound hammer.

On September 8, 1985, after serving seven years and twenty days for the second-degree murder conviction, Streleski was freed unconditionally from prison. According to prison spokesman Joe McGrath, Streleski had been a model prisoner. "He spent most of his time in the library."

But when asked if he felt remorse for committing murder, Streleski said "no"(Associated Press 1985). In his opinion, the murder was "logical and morally correct." It was Streleski's personal protest against "Stanford's inhumane treatment of graduate students." His career goals had been blocked for nineteen years.

Streleski is not an isolated event. In recent years, graduate students have murdered their major professors at other universities, such as the University of Florida, Florida State University, and the University of Iowa.

While Streleski packed his belongings and headed to San Francisco, across the country in Boston, Clinical Psychologist Dr. Joan Ausubel was organizing a long-term support group for graduate students. Referring to the Ph.D. experience as a "grueling process," Dr. Ausubel added, "You can't really understand it if you haven't been through it."

The information in this chapter will help you:

- Understand the process and politics of graduate school.

- Be cognizant of the "hazards" of graduate school.

- Develop communication strategies for coping with the difficult college professors you may encounter in graduate school.

UNDERSTANDING GRADUATE SCHOOL: THE PROCESS

Graduate School—What is it?

Graduate school is a college wherein a student engages in studies beyond the first or bachelor's degree.

What degree or degrees can a student obtain in graduate school?

In graduate school, a student can obtain a master's degree and/or a doctorate degree, commonly known as the Ph.D.

What does "Ph.D." stand for?

It stands for Doctorate of Philosophy.

Is a Ph.D. a medical doctor?

No. Different professions carry specialized degrees. Medical doctors are known as M.D.'s and are not necessarily Ph.D.'s, although a medical doctor can also have obtained a Ph.D.

Does the Ph.D. mean that the person has a doctorate degree in philosophy?
Not usually. It simply means that the person with a Ph.D. is now qualified to "philosophize" (do research) in his or her area of specialization. A person can have a Ph.D. in biology, chemistry, education, or philosophy, for example.

Why do people go to graduate school?
The following lists several reasons for obtaining a graduate degree:

1. In tough economic times, many students find there are limited jobs in their fields which accept only a bachelor's degree. Many attend graduate school, hoping that an advanced degree will better their chances for employment.

2. Some people who have good jobs with their bachelor's degree hope to get promotions or raises within their fields with advanced degrees.

3. In some fields it is mandatory to have an advanced degree. Librarians, for example, are required to hold a master's degree in library science. Many supervisors are also required to have advanced degrees.

4. Many Ph.D.s are hoping to teach and/or do research at a university.

5. Since many people now have bachelor's degrees, the degree has become less valuable. Students often go on to graduate school hoping they'll finally get the credits that will make them unique, outstanding, desirable, and most importantly, employable. Jacob Weisberg (1993) wrote, "Today, paradoxically, a college diploma is considered both essential and nearly meaningless. Since employers can no longer rely on a college diploma per se to have much value, they rely more and more on specialized graduate-school programs to train prospective employees."

How does a student obtain a master's degree? After receiving a bachelor's degree, the student takes an additional year or more of upper-division courses. The student then writes a lengthy research paper, known as a master's thesis. The thesis is periodically critiqued by a professor that the student has selected as an advisor. When this advising professor finds the thesis acceptable, the student graduates. Some master's degree programs do not require the writing of a thesis.

How does a student obtain a doctorate degree?
Obtaining a doctorate degree generally consists of the following steps.

1. The student takes an additional one or two years of coursework beyond the master's degree.

2. After his course is completed, the graduate student must find a professor with whom he will work on a research project or projects. Generally, this professor, known as the student's chairman or advisor, is selected from among the professors with whom the student has taken graduate level courses.

The chairman's job is to oversee the student's research and critique the student's research paper, known as the dissertation.

3. An additional three or four professors are asked by the student to also read and critique the student's dissertation. The chairman and additional professors are known as the student's doctoral committee.

4. Before the student is permitted to conduct a research experiment, he must pass an eight-hour written exam, known as the qualifying exams (sometimes referred to as the *quals*). During that eight hour exam, which is usually divided into two four-hour sessions held on two consecutive days, the student writes several long, detailed essays concerning his or her area of specialization. For example, a student of psychology may be asked to write in detail about every major psychological theory. He may even be asked to advance his own psychological theory and defend it. (Your committee composes the questions.)

5. After this two day exam is complete, the student is then tested orally by his committee members on his comprehensive body of knowledge. If he passes both of these exams, known as written and oral qualifying exams, then his committee gives the student written permission to conduct a research study. After the study is completed, the student writes about what he did, how he did it, and the statistical results he obtained. His committee members critique his research and his research paper until they have determined that the work is satisfactory. When the research paper is completed, (a dissertation is generally about 300 pages long) the professors once again give the student an oral exam. This time they question him about his dissertation results and conclusions. If the student passes this oral examination, known as the *oral defense*, the professors sign his dissertation and the student graduates.

What happens if a student doesn't pass his or her written or oral qualifying exams?

The exams must be taken repeatedly until they are passed. The student cannot go any further in his or her graduate program until these exams have been completed satisfactorily.

What if the student writes a research proposal and his chairman and/or committee do not approve the research idea?

The doctoral committee must approve the dissertation proposal or the student will not be able to continue graduate school. He will have to keep submitting proposals until one is accepted.

What happens if the student completes all the coursework and passes the written and oral qualifying exams, but fails his oral defense?

This is highly unlikely. If the student has completed all but the final oral defense successfully, he will most likely pass. In most cases, the oral defense is simply a formality.

In summary, obtaining a Ph.D. generally consists of ten steps:

1. The student takes an additional one or two years of coursework.

2. A chairman is selected.

3. A committee is formed.

4. The written qualifying exams are taken.

5. The oral qualifying exams are given.

6. A dissertation proposal is submitted to the committee.

7. The student conducts a research study.

8. He writes his dissertation.

9. The student attends an oral defense in which he is questioned by his committee about his research methods, data, results, and conclusions.

10. The committee signs the dissertation and the student graduates with a Ph.D.

UNDERSTANDING THE HAZARDS OF GRADUATE SCHOOL

Most students, prior to entering graduate school, have little or no knowledge about the enormous amount of power professors can exert over graduate students. Knowing these hazards can be helpful in avoiding a situation that may be detrimental to you and your academic career.

Hazard #1: Your chairman determines if and when you graduate. If, for some reason, he dislikes you, he can make sure that you never obtain your doctorate degree.

Frank Herndon was forced to quit graduate school when three members of the sociology department at Fremont State University voted to cancel his assistantship. Herndon's crime? In a nutshell, he had angered two members of his department—a college professor, and the department chairman. Herndon unintentionally upset Professor Nelson by having what the professor considered a light workload for a graduate student. To show his displeasure, Nelson gave Herndon a C, an unacceptable grade in graduate school. Department Chairman Adam Ibsen, advised Herndon to apologize to Nelson to see if the C could be changed to a B. "Why should I apologize when I haven't done anything?" thought Herndon. He decided he'd rather keep the unacceptable C than placate Nelson. The chairman viewed Herndon's noncompliance as a personal insult.

Ibsen told Herndon that the C would oust him from the sociology department, since he had been admitted on probationary status because of low grades in the first place. Knowing this information was against school policy, Herndon demanded that Ibsen call the graduate school immediately and have the matter resolved. Ibsen complied.

But the following semester, Ibsen, Nelson, and one other professor voted that Herndon not receive any more fellowship money. Their reason? Frank Herndon "has a problem communicating," they said. No further explanation was given.

Like Frank Herndon, most graduate students don't realize that getting on the wrong side of a professor can mean the end of their graduate school career.

Another common way that professors try to block students from obtaining their degrees is simply to become very critical of the student's work. "It needs to be redone," the professor tells the student. "What's wrong with my paper as is?" "You figure it out," he replies. "When will I ever graduate?!" the student asks. "I don't know. Whenever this paper is right," he says. This is what happened to Streleski. His chairman told him for nineteen years that his paper was "wrong."

Hazard #2: The student as a pawn. Selecting the wrong professor to chair can mean the end of a student's graduate school career. Feuding between professors is another reason why a graduate student may not obtain his Ph.D. In this scenario, the student is used indirectly to help get rid of a professor whose colleagues wished to oust him but technically could not.

Ri Sing Moon, a Korean, came to the United States to pursue a Ph.D. in political science. He had a reputation for being a bright student and a hard worker. But within a few semesters after being accepted as a graduate student, Moon noticed that he was receiving low or failing grades in all of his classes except those he took with his chairman, *Professor Unwanted*.

How did Ri Sing Moon's low grades help to oust the unwanted professor? First, low grades forced Ri Sing Moon out of the department. Second, without any graduate students to assist, Professor Unwanted had no real responsibility within his department. His two other graduate students were coincidentally also receiving low or failing grades in all their other classes.

Like Moon, most graduate students don't realize that merely picking the wrong professor to chair you can mean the end of your graduate school career.

Hazard #3: Sexual Harrassment. The professor may have agreed to chair you because he wants a sexual relationship with you. You may be expected to be his sweetheart and companion. This is a fairly common practice. One in six women graduate students in psychology reported having sexual intimacy with a professor during their graduate training. An additional thirty percent reported unwanted sexual advances from a professor while in graduate school, according to a survey published in *American Psychologist* (Glaser and Thorpe 1986).

Hazard #4: Professors refusal to give student a good reference. Even if you do graduate, your chairman can still make it virtually impossible for you to obtain a job in higher education. Most professional positions in higher education are obtained through the recommendations and references of your chairman. If he refuses to provide you with a decent reference, you will have a real dilemma. "He will be able to have an influence on her career opportunities for the rest of his life," said Anne Truax of the University of Minnesota.

Hazard #5: The professor using the student's work to further his own career. Your chairman may have agreed to chair you to boost his own career. Some professors' careers are jeopardized because they are short on published articles. Your chairman may have agreed to chair you so that you will publish your dissertation as a research article, with his name as senior author. In other words, you do all the work, but he takes primary credit.

Hazard #6: Chair drops the project. If your chairman decides to stop chairing you, you may not be able to obtain another advisor, and consequently, you won't be able to receive your degree. A professor's decision to stop chairing you may come as a total surprise to you. There is no way to prepare for such an event. It is another example of the capricious, whimsical, and arbitrary use of power granted to professors in higher education.

Paula C., a Ph.D. candidate in mathematics from Italy, was eager to complete her graduate studies. She was hard-working, brilliant, and diligent. One day, while working on her dissertation, her chairman announced, "I have decided I no longer want to chair you." (This is a privilege professors have. They face no consequences for making such a whimsical decision.)

Flabbergasted, she demanded to know why. "Just not interested," he replied, with a shrug."Then, what am I to do!?" Paula declared. "I don't know. It's not my problem," he replied. "Find another chairman. Or go back to Italy."

No explanation was even given for the professor's behavior. It was certainly not a reflection of her work. After approaching every professor in the math department and being turned down, Paula returned to Italy. Before departing, Paula said, "The time and money I spent working toward obtaining a Ph.D. were, in effect, a complete waste of my time."

Hazard #7: Job scarcity. There is a glut of Ph.D.'s. Having a Ph.D. is no guarantee that you will be able to find a job in higher education. Even in the best fields, there are far more people with advanced degrees than there are job openings.

Dr. Zoran Pop'Stojanovic, professor of mathematics at the University of Florida, said his department received nearly 2,000 applications when a position recently opened up in his department. Mathematics is considered to be one of the more lucrative fields.

Emily K. Abel, author of *Terminal Degrees: The Job Crisis In Higher Education* (1984), wrote,

... as the job market for both high school and college graduates deteriorates, it becomes increasingly clear that schools are not the magical path to the good life. . . . In short, it is doubtful that the academic job crisis is simply a temporary phenomenon.

Hazard #8: Some professors violate the first amendment of the U.S. Constitution—freedom of speech—and there is little you can do about it. Because of their enormous power, professors can stop chairing you if you simply express ideas contrary to their own. In *Robots in the Classroom*, Jane Bergen (1986) quotes a fellow graduate student's advice to her when she first entered graduate school,

> Now, I'm not trying to scare you, Jane Balek. I just don't want to see you get hurt. If you taught at Westhaven, you have to be good. You are high quality and you look it. You are not the kind to fawn and flatter, and that is the chief requirement for a Ph.D. ... And if you expect to get one, you had better begin kowtowing now. . . if you want a degree you must agree with everything she [the chairperson] says.

COMMUNICATION STRATEGIES

So what can you do to help guarantee that the hazards don't happen to you?

1. *Check out the reputation of the professor.*

Talk with other graduate students. Contact graduates who were chaired by him. Find out what he was like to work with. Did he help them obtain a job after graduation? Does he use students to boost his own career? If you are a woman, find out if his previous graduate assistants had been women/lovers? If there's a professor you trust, ask him/her about the reputation of the professor in question. Does he seem to care about students? How much time does he spend helping a student compose the dissertation? Is he available for good critiques, or is he frequently out of town?

2. *Have a long talk with the professor in advance.*

Ask him what he expects from his graduate students. And listen. Really listen. Does he tend to get off on tangents or ask you a lot of irrelevant personal questions about your love life? What has he published? What is his status in the department? Will you be assisting with his own research, or will he allow you to do your own thing? How often does he like to meet with students he's sponsoring? Does he seem content with what he is doing?

3. Read the research he's published.

If he's an expert in his field, well-respected around the world for what he's doing, it will be much easier for him to find you a job. People who interview you will be much more impressed to discover that you worked under such a distinguished professor. If, on the other hand, he hasn't published anything since 1956, he probably does not have much clout as far as getting you a decent job in academia after you graduate.

There is a balance, however. Sometimes the most distinguished professors have high expectations of those they agree to chair. If he is very well known, you must find out in advance what he expects from graduate students and whether or not he relates to his graduate students in strictly a professional manner.

SUMMARY

In 1957 four graduate deans, Jacques Barzun of Columbia University, John Petersen Edler of Harvard University, Marcus Hobbs of Duke University, and Andrew Robertson Gordon of the University of Toronto (1957), spoke out against the hazards of graduate school in *Time* magazine. Little has changed since then; their words could have been written yesterday.

Getting the Ph.D. is tortuously slow and riddled with needless uncertainties . . . it is frequently inefficient and tramatically disagreeable to the frustrated candidate . . . Too many men emerge from this ordeal spiritually dried up . . . The desire for finding out what had not been known, the imaginative urge to reinterpret—these the tired and weary student has gradually lost. He has been wrung dry, and knowlingly or not, he often finishes his thesis with the firm resolve to have no more to do with scholarship . . . Nor is the emerging Ph.D. what we mean by an educated man, a man who combines wide-range learning with an attitude of simplicity and vividness, and who commingles good taste with excited curiosity. Rather, he likely has become a sort of expert plumber in the card catalogues . . . and neither as a teacher nor scholar will he throw off this inhibiting heritage.

Many students imagine graduate school as a time " . . . of blissful learning at the feet of scholars and of congenial companionship with peers," wrote Peter Lowenberg, author of *Decoding the Past* (1983). Lowenberg claims that the graduate school experience is one that leaves the graduate with one of two experiences—either a very positive experience, " . . . a journey of growth, self-realization, intellectual independence, and autonomy," or a very negative, damaging experience " . . . ending in bitterness, cynicism, and disillusionment," depending upon how the major professor and/or committee interacted with the graduate student on an emotional level.

In May 1995, an article appearing in *Mademoiselle* magazine asked the question: *Do graduate degrees really increase your salary by as much as fifteen percent?* The article states, "Nothing is certain . . . M.B.A.'s don't even guarantee jobs, much less instant high salaries . . . A graduate degree can, however, increase your long-term earning potential. Check out *U.S. News & World Report Guide to America's Best Graduate Schools*, which lists starting salaries for recent graduates according to degree and school."

The purpose of this chapter was to make you aware of the hazards of graduate school so you will be more likely to have a successful, productive experience. Naive students are those most likely to be victimized. It's much better to enter a situation "with both eyes open."

11

What Colleges Don't Want You To Know

Parents are scared stiff that they won't be able to afford their children's college education. Tuition rates are rising twice as fast as inflation and student aid is increasingly difficult to obtain. It has been estimated that a decade from now, a single year at a state university will cost about $10,000. At a private college, the cost could be about three times higher. Fearful that they won't be able to support their sons' and daughters' college education, many parents are opening college savings accounts for their grade school children.

Underlying the fear is a basic belief that college is a worthwhile investment. "Going to college has become generally accepted as essential in the fulfillment of [the American] dream," wrote Emma Coburn Norris, *Chronicle of Higher Education* (1985).

When entering college, freshmen were asked by the *Chronicle of Higher Education* (Nasrin 1989) why they had decided to attend college. More than three-fourths listed "to be able to get a better job" and "to be able to make more money" as essential reasons. With such a strong underlying belief that college is the launching pad for financial success, it is no wonder that many parents report they are scared stiff about not being able to afford their sons' and daughters' future college education.

But is it true? Is a bachelor's degree such a dire necessity that parents should spend their entire life's savings (as some have reportedly done), take out a second mortgage on their homes, or take on additional jobs just to fund their child's college education? Does everyone need a college degree?

After studying job forecasts and academic trends for more than a decade, examining the history of higher education, and discovering that it has been only in the past three decades that Americans have come to believe that "everyone needs a college degree," I am convinced that people do not necessarily need college degrees to succeed economically. In fact, I believe there are several strong, valid reasons why parents should consider alternatives to the expensive, four/five year bachelor's degree.

1. A majority of jobs do not require a four-year college degree (Littwin 1986).

2. Forty percent of college graduates work at jobs that do not require higher education (Weisberg 1993).

3. A majority of jobs in the future will require two years of post-secondary training or less, not a four year college degree.

4. This expensive "rite of passage" often postpones adulthood.

5. The liberal arts, per se, no longer exist.

Most Jobs Don't Require a College Degree

Darrell Baker is described as a good, "all-American boy," by one of his co-workers. Ten years ago, he sold his home, quit his job as a used car salesman, and decided to go to college. His dream was to become a top sales representative for a large, prestigious corporation. "I had always envied people with college degrees," Baker said. "I wanted to go back to school so I could be treated more fairly. I wanted to be more successful."

Ten years later, with a business administration degree in hand, Darrell Baker is back in the used car business. After interviews with several major companies for sales rep positions, Baker learned one thing: a college degree does not provide an automatic ticket to success. With a $4,000 student loan debt still facing him, Baker said, "I spent about $40,000 during those four years of college. I sold a home I'll probably never be able to afford ever again at today's prices. And I don't think large corporations treat their employees any better than I get treated as a used car salesman. I'm definitely more cynical."

Baker is just one of four million college graduates who can't find degree-related employment following graduation, according to the

Bureau of Labor Statistics (BLS) as quoted in California researcher Russell W. Rumberger's report *Education, Unemployment and Productivity* (1983).

"It's a real problem," said a Florida employment counselor. "There's a great deal of them who come in here and think that a college degree alone will get them a high-paying, professional job. I feel sorry for them. Many of them end up as waiters and waitresses."

Projections show that nearly 26 million college graduates will enter the labor force between 1986 and 2,000—an average of 1,850,000 per year. About 900,000 of these annual entrants will be new college graduates. They will compete with unemployed and underemployed college graduates for jobs that require a college degree. But an average of 100,000 graduates annually will work in jobs that don't require a college education, in jobs such as retail sales, service, blue collar jobs, and administrative support. This does not imply that the economy will not grow between now and the end of the century. Indeed, it is projected that there will be about 150,000 new job openings per year, which indicates a modest but steady growth rate. But most of the new jobs do not require post secondary schooling and will pay wages significantly lower than the average.

"There will be three times as many new jobs for janitors as jobs for computer-system analysts," wrote Rumburger, "and there will be 13 times as many jobs for waiters and waitresses as jobs for aeronautical engineers."

Claudia Underwood, Employment Service Representative, Chicago, said,

It appears that most of them [college students] . . . are very enthusiastic about getting into whatever field they have majored in, whatever that field may be. And then once they get out and actually start looking for work, they gradually become more disappointed, more disillusioned. They're going around and they're being told, 'We're looking for experience.' And some of them have no experience. They have various problems that they didn't foresee. They obviously were not counseled or guided toward facing the world of work upon completion of college. And the longer they are unemployed, the more disappointed they become.

Many of them end up majoring in one field and then looking for some other. In other words, they end up lowering their sights. For instance, there are a lot of people who have been advised and are majoring in business; we have a great deal going into business administration and communications. That's the going thing now.

When they get out, what they're finding is that those fields are highly competitive—they are highly competitive—and some of them are just not up to it in many cases, and some of them are just not able to compete.

Some of them are saying, 'Why did I go to college? I did this for what? My parents told me that if I got a good education I would get a good job. And now look at me. I was advised to go to school and get an education and that the doors would be opened to me, and it's not happening.' I'm hearing this message in some form or another.

Some people come in here with a degree and think just because I have this degree I'm going to get this job. But they don't realize there's other people out there with degrees, too. So, they have to be told that this world is highly competitive. It's not enough just to have a degree. You have to be super, as super as you can be. Business and journalism and communications are overcrowded fields. And some of the jobs which are in greatest demand—secretary, waitress, retail sales—the college grad feels those jobs are beneath him.

Sometimes they feel kind of betrayed. They say, 'I wanted to get married and my parents told me to stay in school so that I could get this good job and make this money and now here am I? I didn't get married and I don't have a good job.'

A study conducted by the U.S. Department of Labor in New York concluded that many employers are arbitrarily raising job requirements to accommodate the spillover of college graduates.

In 1978, about 250,000 New York State college graduates worked in occupations that in 1970, did not require a college education. Of these, 42 percent were in jobs not traditionally sought by college graduates. This proportion is expected to rise . . . The percentage of total job openings in New York State for those with a high school diploma should rise; the smallest gain should occur in the college graduate classification.

Even more disturbing is a statement published in the *Chronicle of Higher Education* by Harold Howe II, the chairman of the Grant Foundation Commission, "High school graduates are finding themselves in the same jobs as high school drop-outs." Howe also noted that America is increasingly becoming a service-oriented society and that "salaries for new jobs in services and related sectors were half those paid for typical manufacturing jobs." This information implies that many college graduates, high school graduates, and high school drop-outs are working the same low-paying jobs.

Is High Tech The Answer?

Many parents advise their college-bound children to major in high tech fields. But high technology is not expected to dominate the future job market. Only one million new high tech jobs, which is less than four percent of all new jobs, will become available in the 1982-1995 period. Occupations that will experience the fastest growth require little or no college training.

The greatest number of new jobs will be for building custodians, cashiers, secretaries, general clerks, waitresses, truck drivers, nurses aides, and orderlies. There are two fields, presently, which need more bachelor's degree recipients—teaching and nursing.

But the high tech field, according to Richard McGahey of New York University's Urban Research Center (1990), has "bottomed out." Last year, there were "52,000 college graduates competing for 24,000 entry-level jobs in computer programming," he said.

John Hill of the *Gainesville Sun* states, "According to U.S. Census projections, the fastest-decliining occupations over the next decade will be in computer, telephone and skilled office jobs."(1995)

High technology may displace both non-skilled and skilled workers in such large numbers that the U.S. economy may not be able to generate enough new jobs, according to Rumberger (1984). For example, a recent study suggests that robots may eliminate 100,000 to 200,000 jobs, while creating only 32,000 to 64,000 new jobs. These figures imply that anywhere from 67,000 to 167,000 jobs will be permanently lost without replacement due to the use of robotics.

Is a Business Major The Answer?

Business has become a very popular college major. In fact, twenty-five percent of this year's entering freshman selected business as their career choice, hoping that an MBA (Masters in Business Administration) will guarantee them management positions with large, prestigious corporations.

But there is already a growing surplus of MBA's who don't quite make it as top executives for Fortune 500 companies. Instead, they end up as manager trainees in fast food restaurants, clothing stores, and discount retail outlets. These jobs do not necessarily require a college education. MBA's find themselves competing for supervisory positions with high school graduates. And who will get promoted—the MBA or the high school graduate with six years of on-the-job-experience?

"I find the college graduates frequently come across as arrogant, even hostile, toward customers," said one fast food supervisor. "They feel they should be starting off somewhere higher because they have a college degree. I don't promote them."

A Sanford, Florida employment counselor said part of his job is to help young people cope with the depression they feel after getting a college degree and not being able to find degree-related employment. "I help them cope with their feelings of low self-worth," he said. "It's a real blow to their egos."

"Most of them feel they're going to be the exception to the rule," said another counselor. "They get mad at me when I tell them I don't have anything for them. They say, 'But I have a college degree,' thinking that's really going to make a difference."

One MBA recipient who worked as an appliance salesman for Sears prior to college, said, "I went on a job interview at the University of Florida Career Resource Center for a hotel sales rep position. But the personnel director insulted me. I left five minutes into the interview. She wanted me to start working at $16,000 per year and I told her I could make more than that working part-time in commission sales at Sears."

"My daughter is one of the 'overeducated,'" said a mother who works for the Red Cross in Sanford, Florida. "She got a degree in criminal justice and is now working in a gift shop at EPCOT. I used to think it was just my daughter but now I realize it's a lot of young people."

Darrell Baker said he feels the college experience made him lose confidence in himself. "Being back where I started before I got a college degree is pretty much of an ego blow. I feel I'm turning into one of those people I never wanted to be—just an average kind of guy who goes to work, and does an average kind of job. The college experience, in its totality, was probably a pretty big mistake for me."

FUTURE JOBS—WILL A BACHELOR'S DEGREE BE NEEDED?

Many parents appear unconcerned with the present glut of college educated people. Many continue to believe that they need to send their children to college because there will be a greater demand for the college educated in the future. In the future, they reason, there will be more technology and therefore, there will be greater demand for highly educated people.

Futurist Magazine predicted the following new jobs will be in demand in the 1990's: energy technician, housing rehabilitation technician, hazardous waste management technician, genetic engineering technician, holographic inspection specialist, bionic-electronic technician, battery technician, paramedic,and geriatric social worker. Only two of these jobs require a costly four-year college education: bionic-electronic technician and geriatric social worker.

The other new jobs, mostly technical in nature, will require a high school diploma and two years of technical post-secondary training. Employers will prefer to hire those who have less academic training and more on-the-job experience. In a highly technical society where technology is constantly and rapidly changing, employers will not want to hire people who have spent four to six years of time in college. By the time they graduate, much of what they learned in a technical field will be obsolete.

Many large companies are now offering the "corporate B.A." Corporations are taking the brightest high school graduates, paying them while training them, and guaranteeing them a secure job. These students bypass paying $15,000 a year for a college education, and instead *earn while they learn.* "It is only a question of time," wrote Dean Herbert London (1987) before the corporate B.A. is perceived as a direct competitor to the conventional college degree.

HOW COLLEGE PROFESSORS SPEND THEIR TIME

James Ridgeway, author of *The Closed Corporation* (1968), writes:

In all likelihood most Americans believe that a university is a place where professors teach students. They are wrong. In fact, the university looks more like a center for industrial activity than a community of scholars.

Universities are now operated by teams of management executives, who often see themselves as labor mediators. They run what in effect is a kind of data-processing center: part bank, to provide the money for the activities of the different subsidiaries; part brokerage, for arranging deals among quarreling faculty members or between a faculty group and the government. The undergraduates, for their part, lie in holding pens, off the labor market, providing the rationale for financing the university. The older graduate students, of course, provide cheap labor pools, useful for keeping the undergraduates in hand and for assisting the senior professors in carrying forward their inquiries both within the university or in some private company.

Ridgeway claims that products, or processes, are conceived by the university, then funded by the state or federal government, and ultimately used or sold by private industry. Professors dart back and forth between writing government grants and developing new products for private industry. Tuition monies and government monies are used to fund the development of products for profit-making corporations.

Charles J. Sykes says, in his book *Profscam* (1988), that college teaching has degenerated into a huge, highly successful racket. He maintains that college professors generally ignore their most important responsibility—teaching—in favor of research and designing profit-making products.

- Gatorade, for example, is a beverage that was developed by a University of Florida professor which is now distributed for profit by the Van Camp Corporation.

- The professor who developed the very popular Rotation Diet, Dr. Martin Katahn, Vanderbilt University, has teamed up with other large corporations, such as Publix and Wendy's, for the promotion of his weight loss plan.

- Ernest W. Brewer, University of Tennessee, developed a monopoly-type game, "Political Challenge," which he's attempting to promote to national game companies.

- The University of West Virginia is promoting its newly developed beverage, Mountaineer Cola, and hopes to compete on a large scale with the Pepsi-Cola and Coca-Cola corporations.

- Dr. James J. Buergermeister, University of Wisconsin, has spent a lot of time at his publicly-funded job as a college professor developing a turkeyburger for the Burger King corporation.

Having university professors develop products is a lot cheaper for corporations than having their own laboratories, since professors are paid by the state and conduct experiments in state-funded facilities.

There are universities that own motels, ball parks, ships, real estate, and newspapers. The University of Wisconsin, for example, manufactures the world's leading rat poison. NYU owns a spaghetti factory. According to Ridgeway, it is consistently rumored (but reports denied), that Yale is in the bra business.

The more students a college can enroll, the more money it has to invest—just like any large corporation—in stocks, property, and business ventures.

THE SELLING OF HIGHER EDUCATION THROUGH THE PROMOTION OF THE LIBERAL ARTS

Beginning in the late 1970's universities became very concerned with the fact that baby-boomers were graduating and less young people would be available to enroll in colleges. During the 1960s, an average of one community college per week was built in the United States. Now, many are afraid that they will have to close their doors. Many colleges and universities, aware that bachelor's degrees don't necessarily lead to the graduate finding degree-related employment, have taken a new strategy for promoting higher education.

There is a belief that college-educated people are well-rounded, knowledgeable, and therefore better suited for leadership positions in the community; that they are more open-minded, more flexible, and more tolerant of differences because of their college education. The specific aspect of education that supposedly endows college graduates with such depth and breadth of character is the liberal arts curriculum required for a bachelor's degree. This is composed of courses in humanities, literature, music, art, social sciences, philosophy, history, and psychology. When William J. Bennett was the Secretary of Education, he identified the liberal arts as "a body of knowledge and a means of inquiry that convey serious truths, defensible judgments, and significant ideas."

Every college student's career begins with a mandatory two years of liberal arts courses.

According to a University of Florida catalog,

> The major aim of the College [of liberal arts] is to impart the ideas, concepts, motivations, and skills of a liberal education to

its students to enable them to assume leadership positions in society. Intellectual inquiry, the intelligent evaluation of ideas, and an appreciation of the dominant thought patterns of the world are the tools that the college insists its graduates possess. Upon these fundamentals they can build personally rewarding lives and careers.

It sounds good, doesn't it? In an article that appeared in the *Independent Florida Alligator* (1990) a panel of University of Florida educators said,

> The purpose of a college education is to make students intellectually mature, not to get them jobs . . . too many people go to college for the wrong reasons. Most people come to college to get a degree they think will lead to a job.

So, in tough economic times, the promotion of the Liberal Arts keeps the public sold on the idea of obtaining a college degree.

Questionable Curriculum Criteria

In America, the original purpose of a liberal arts education was to help people understand and freely adopt the morals and values of Western civilization. In order to accomplish this objective, colleges made it mandatory that their students take a uniform set of liberal arts courses based upon the most popular books that have influenced the thinking of our leaders through history.

Known as the 'Great Books', they include the works of such authors as St. Thomas Acquinas, Shakespeare, and Thomas Payne. An understanding of the U.S. Constitution and a reading of the Federalist Papers was also included as part of the mandatory liberal arts core curriculum that all students used to take.

Beginning in the turbulent 1960s, young people argued that they wanted to be free to take their own custom-designed liberal arts program rather than be forced to read only the Great Books. Colleges, concerned with enrollments and money, complied. Today, liberal arts can be anything from a course called "Fun With Jell-O", (a liberal arts course which shows how much one can do with Jell-O), to "Film Genres", a course in which students can quote magazines like *Teen Beat* for doing papers on their favorite rock stars, like Madonna.

In another popular liberal arts offering, "Personal Growth and Development", students learn about New Age principles via an American professor who comes to class clad in Eastern Indian get-up. He wears a pendant around his neck depicting a photograph of his favorite Indian guru, a frequent reference in his lectures. Part of the course requirements includes going to a singles bar and asking someone to dance, so that students will lose their "hang-ups." The course concludes with the writing of a paper on "how personal growth and development changed my life." Woe to the student who claims it didn't.

Even more traditional sounding courses, such as "Shakespeare in Literature" may take an untraditional approach. A male professor of literature identified himself as a "radical feminist" and required his students to scrutinize passages from Shakespeare for evidence of sexism.* Another professor, who teaches a course called "Survey of Learning Theories" discussed only one learning theory throughout the entire semester—his favorite theory, the one he researches for publication purposes.

The liberal arts curriculum sounds well and good, as described in course catalogs, and higher education administrators tend to discuss the liberal arts as strictly a curriculum. But inside that curriculum are real people, college professors, who deliver whatever 'truths', under the guise of academic freedom, they wish to promote. There are professors who openly identify themselves as counter-culture in their beliefs and they slant liberal arts courses to reflect their own values. "It is not a gross exaggeration to suggest that the student radical of yesteryear is now a tenured professor," wrote Dean Herbert London (1987).

Today, the vast majority of liberal arts courses do not reflect or enhance traditional values. Universities now offer such a large choice of liberal arts courses that a student can graduate without ever having taken a single course in the classics, the U.S. Constitution, or Western Civilization.

In the 1970s, Harvard tried to reinstate a mandatory 'core' liberal arts curriculum—about 150 courses from which a student can select liberal arts offerings. But *Time* magazine noted (1987), "Little and scattered is what many educators feel Harvard's core provides. The University of Massachusetts' Duffey describes its effect on learning as modest. Harvard, he says, does not 'seem any closer to making judgments about the qualities of an educated mind.'"

---

*The purpose of a liberal education in the past was to provide the learner with several theories and philosophies to think about—not to proselytize.

ALTERNATIVES TO COLLEGE

William J. Bennett suggested that parents take the $40,000 they would have spent on their child's four year college degree and instead set up their offspring in business for him or herself. I don't think that's a bad idea. Perhaps America's degree obsession will pass and people will start believing that they can perform without a college degree.

Meanwhile, I have some other suggestions and recommendations:

1. When a college representative takes you on a tour of his college or visits your high school and shows a flashy videotape presentation of life at his university, don't automatically think that everything he is telling you about the value of a college degree reflects the current job market for college graduates. His goal is to recruit students.

If enrollments are too low, his institution will lose government research grant monies, investment monies, and clout. Double check with the U.S. Department of Labor when a college counselor tells you "everybody ends up getting a job when they graduate." (A college admissions officer at a large southeastern university told me exactly that a few years ago. He didn't mention that some of those jobs that "everybody" gets include flipping hamburgers and scrubbing toilet bowls.)

2. Read between the lines when you see a rosy article in your local newspaper about the wonderful job prospects for college graduates. "Optimistic over economic growth, businesses will significantly increase their hiring of college graduates in 1988 and also will boost starting salaries, says a Northwestern University survey." This was the opening paragraph of an Associated Press (1987) news release that appeared in several newspapers across the nation. Ask yourself, "How can it be that businesses are optimistic and will hire more people given that we are in a major recession?" Ask yourself, "How were those statistics determined?" A few years ago I seriously investigated this matter and here's what I discovered:

There are a number of public relations (PR) agencies in the United States that write PR pieces for universities, based on a university's statistics. How does the university get its statistics?

The university sends out questionnaires to its graduates asking what kinds of employment they have found. The graduate fills out the form and lists "cocktail waitress" as her post-graduate job. She has a degree in psychology. Another graduate reports, "I work as a typesetter for a newspaper." She holds a bachelor's degree in journalism. A third writes, "I'm back at home living with my parents. I do a little bit of writing and drawing. I'm trying to get my work published. I've been accepted to start graduate school in the fall." He has a degree in English.

How does the university deal with these embarrassing statistics? The placement officers create broad, general catagories for these graduates. One catagory is "Hotels, Motels, Resorts, and Resturants." The placement officer lists the cocktail waitress under this category. Another category is "Printing, Publishing, and Advertising." The journalism graduate who works as a typesetter is placed under this category. The third graduate, who dabbles with art and writing, may be placed under one of several different categoes. He may be enumerated under "Art, Drama, and Related Arts;" or he may be chronicled under "Graduate School." (About 50% of bachelors degree recipients are now chronicled under this category). Some universities claim they don't keep any statistics on their graduates. Some say they only document the whereabouts of their engineers and computer programmers.

These statistics are then sent into one of the public relations firms whose job is to write rosy press releases for universities that appear in newspaper articles across the country. The PR agency writes, "92 percent of all college graduates were employed within three months after graduation." Technically, the information is correct. As the admission officer said, "Everybody gets a job."

In April 1995, an Associated Press article appearing in the *Gainesville Sun* examined contentions that some colleges, "under pressure to attract students, are fibbing about the figures they send each year for the rankings done by *U.S. News & World Report, Money* magazine and others." The article elaborates on a *Wall Street Journal* article, appearing earlier in the same month, which reported the discovery of descrepancies in data sent for the rankings, and information sent to debt-rate agencies. SAT scores were frequently reflected as flawed data. The article quotes:

Lee Stetson, dean of admissions at the University of Pennsylvania, as saying "It's a buyer's market and the amount of publicity you get helps determine the students you get." "Some of these schools admitted to purposely lying on our survey," says Robert Morse, director of research for the U.S. News guide. The same colleges "would reject a student who lied on an application." "The difference between ranking No. 1 and No. 2 in one of these surveys is simply not a credible difference," said Barbara-Jan Wilson, dean of admissions and financial aid at Wesleyan University in Middletown, Connecticut. "Nevertheless, its a wonderful marketing tool for the school ranked No.1."

3. If your child is resistant to the idea of attending college, listen to him or her. There is a good chance that this child will not work his hardest in college. He may switch majors a dozen times and earn grades that are so low that employers will be reluctant to hire him.

Tom received C's and D's in computer sciences, his major. He felt that the computer degree alone would guarantee him a good job. Three years after graduation he found employment as a technical writer for a large aircraft corporation. During the four years he was with the firm, before they closed their doors, he repeatedly made formal requests to be transferred to the computer department. Now, in another company, also as a technical writer, he has made the same request, but he recently learned that the company plans a hiring freeze. Tom feels increasingly certain that he will never be employed as a computer programmer.

4. Look into the possibility of sending your child to a community college instead of a university. Think of the advantages. In two years or less your son or daughter will have a marketable skill and will be able to earn a living, instead of postponing adulthood earning endless degrees. Computer repair graduates, for example, obtain starting salaries around $30,000.

Think of the advantages this individual has. With such earning power he can now go back to college, if he chooses, and earn as many college degrees as he wants without being a financial burden to his parents. And there won't be any huge student loan debts facing him.

In a recent survey, it was estimated that one in five high school students plans to attend a two-year technical or junior college after graduation instead of a four-year university.

5. If the college tells you there's a surplus of graduates in your field of interest, listen to them. Don't think to yourself, "Oh, that doesn't really matter. I'm smart and I'm different. Two million others might not get a job in this field, but I certainly will."

A college professor told a young woman who was pursuing a degree in political science, "If your grades are good enough, you'll be able to get a job as a political science researcher for the Defense Department." After graduation, with good grades in hand, this young woman made a special trip to Washington, D.C., to impress government officials, in person, with her credentials. She was shocked to discover that even to get an internship with the Defense Department required a master's degree and two years' experience working for a local law enforcement agency. Now she is an assistant manager at a clothing store at a local mall.

6. Consider the institution's reputation. If the university sent you a letter of acceptance and you never even applied (Yes! This has really happened, see *Emory* magazine, December, 1985). assume they're hurting for enrollees. Have a couple of companies in mind for whom you'd like to work after graduation. Call them up. Ask them, "From which universities do you recruit new employees?" If "Big State University" isn't one of them, consider switching to another college.

The old saying that "a college degree alone will make the difference" no longer applies. In the 1960s, that may have been true, but it's now the 1990s and everyone bought the idea that a college degree can make a difference. Today, job experience and communication skills is what's making the difference.

SUMMARY

The purpose of this chapter was to give you a balanced view of higher education. Throughout high school and college, teachers, parents, guidance counselors, and the like, have only presented the *benefits* of college to you. You have heard repeatedly that you won't make it in life without a college degree. You have also heard that the only way to get a real education is to go to college. The purpose of this chapter was to add the other side to the body of knowledge you already have regarding information you've heard about college.

I was under the impression that by now, almost all entering college freshman were aware of the bleak outlook for college graduates, regarding degree-related employment. But just the other day, I was having lunch at an outdoor cafe in Gainesville, Florida. The waitress had just received her bachelor's degree six months ago and was still working as a waitperson at a vegetarian cafe. "Didn't you realize how scarce the degree-related jobs are for college graduates?" I asked her.

"Yes, I was aware," she replied, but I didn't think it was *that* bad and I certainly didn't think it would happen to *me*." I have casually interviewed, another 300 who sound just like her, and I am just as baffled as they are that they (a) do not comprehend that there really are very few

PART III

Sexual Harrassment

12

Coping with Sexual Harassment

According to university research (Till 1980), about ninety-eight percent of all sexual harassment happens to women. But sexual harassment is really a problem that affects everyone in our society. When a difficult teacher makes sexist remarks in front of the class, he is harassing all his students—not just the female students.

This important chapter is divided into three sections. In the first part, you'll learn exactly what sexual harassment is. The second part includes ten case studies from women who have experienced sexual harassment. The third section lists four sets of remedies for dealing with sexual harassment; individual, institutional, departmental, and legal recourse.

UNDERSTANDING SEXUAL HARASSMENT:
NO JOKING MATTER

Mary walked into the university counseling center and said she was feeling tired, angry, upset, and anxious. She had also been experiencing gastrointestinal disturbances, headaches, insomnia, weight loss, and crying spells.

At first, Mary had difficulty defining what was wrong with her. Her work load at school was not overly burdensome, and she wasn't having any trouble with her boyfriend. When pressed further, the only problem she could think of was with a professor she was assisting frequently. But his behavior didn't seem like that big of a problem.

As the counseling sessions continued, Mary described how the professor made constant unwelcomed and unwanted comments about her physical attractiveness. He frequently cracked derogatory "jokes" about women. Recently, he had begun to "accidentally" brush up against her. Prior to counseling, Mary had described the professor's behavior to a few close friends who replied, "Oh, Mary, lighten up. Have a sense of humor." After that, Mary ignored him. She convinced herself that it was probably her imagination that he was trying to touch her. But after several months of therapy Mary was able to clearly articulate what she had been experiencing: she was a victim of sexual harassment.

Every day students across the nation describe the symptoms of sexual harassment to counselors. Few, however, link the term *sexual harassment* to the symptoms. Despite media attention, a plethora of newspaper articles (including the Anita Hill case), sexual harassment remains a seriously misunderstood experience, according to Michele Paludi, editor of *Ivory Power: Sexual Harassment on Campus* (1990).

> One of the most difficult issues that I find in training students, faculty, or administrators around the country is that individuals believe that unless you've been physially assaulted you haven't been sexually harassed . . . And yet the research that we and other colleagues around the country have done with students and with women employees suggests that the most common forms of harassment are the "hostile environment" type—the seductive comments, the sexist comments, the demeaning statements about women's performance and women's bodies. These are the most commonly experienced forms of sexual harassment.

Many people, like Mary's friends, perceive these forms of sexual harassment as minor incidents to be ignored. Bombarded frequently with sexual innuendos, negative comments about females, and "jokes" about women and their bodies, it is no wonder that so many people think of sexual harassment as normal behavior to be overlooked.

In 1972, the United States Supreme Court decided that sexual harassment was not a joking matter. According to Title IX of the Higher Education Amendments of 1972, there are two forms of sexual harassment. A victim can wage a formal complaint with the Equal Employment Opportunity Commission or bring legal suit against anyone who engages in either form of sexual harassment.

Quid pro quo is a Latin phrase which literally means "this for that." It is easier for an attorney to build a legal case around this type of harassment because it is basically extortion. The professor who says, "If you don't have sex with me, I won't give you a passing grade," or, "I'll withhold good evaluations," or, "I won't give you a job reference," is engaging in quid pro quo. About twenty percent of college women experience this form of sexual harassment during their college years. Researchers say the long-term aftereffects of quid pro quo sexual harassment are very similar to those experienced by rape and incest victims.

Many victims suffer from Post-Traumatic Stress Disorder (PTSD), the very serious disease first attributed to emotionally traumatized Vietnam veterans. Most professors these days are too "hip" to engage in blatant quid pro quo. Instead, they give the student the very indirect message, "Put out or get out."

Here's how it works. Professor X asks a coed to work with him because she is so bright. He begins commenting frequently on her attractiveness. Soon, he is inviting her to lunch, then to dinner. At first, unsuspecting, she is flattered by her professor's attentiveness. By the time she catches on to his true motives, although never directly spoken, she feels intimidated. She worries about her future career. She graciously declines dates. He, in turn, lowers her grade for a "justified" reason. It's quid pro quo.

According to one of two pamphlets on sexual harassment published by Hunter College (1990), sexual harassment isn't really about sex or sexual desire—it's about power.

> It is a breach of the trust that normally exists between students and others in the academic community. Sexual harassment creates confusion because the boundary between professional roles and personal relationships is blurred. The harasser introduces a sexual element into an academic setting where it has no place. Put simply, sexual harassment is any coerced, unethical, and unwanted emphasis on sexuality or gender.

The two Hunter College pamphlets list the following as examples of sexual harassment:

- Forcing unwanted sexual attention, such as sexually suggestive comments

- Attempting to coerce you into a sexual relationship

- Threatening punishment for refusal to comply with sexual advances

- Implying that sexual favors may be a basis for grades in a course or otherwise influencing your academic career

- Engaging in conduct of a sexual nature which has the purpose or effect of interfering with your performance in class or creating an intimidating, hostile, or offensive working or learning environment

- Propositioning sexual invitations, or other pressuring for sex. These might include insistent invitations for drinks, dinner, dates, and uninvited visits to your hotel room during conferences

- Patting, pinching, brushing up against the body, and any other inappropriate touching or feeling such as attempted or actual kissing or fondling

- Assault and rape

- Leering or ogling

- Obscene gestures and obvious sexual gestures

- Offensive graffiti

- Threats of physical assault

- Sending lewd cartoons, cards, presents, or letters

The second form of sexual harassment, known as the *hostile environment,* is much more difficult for an attorney to build a legal case for. About seventy percent of women are exposed to this form of sexual harassment—sexual innuendos, jokes, derogatory comments, and the like.

It's illegal because it makes people nervous; it stresses them out. When people have to work or learn under unduly stressful conditions, it lowers the quality of their work. Also, if women learn to "tune out" the comments, there's a good chance that more serious forms of sexual harassment will occur, such as pinching, patting, squeezing, touching, and asking for sexual favors. This form of sexual harassment is also known as *gender harassment.* Here are some examples listed by Hunter College:

- Disparaging women's intellectual abilities and potential

- Disparaging women's seriousness of academic commitment

- Using sexist humor as a classroom teaching technique

- Turning a discussion of a woman student's work into a discussion of her physical attributes or appearance

- Disparaging scholarly works by or about women

- Ridiculing specific works because they deal with women's perceptions and/or feelings

COMMON REACTIONS TO SEXUAL HARASSMENT

Hunter College lists the following as common reactions to harassment:

- Changing college or graduate school major

- Leaving job, college, or city

- Becoming depressed, anxious, losing of self-esteem

- Suffering from headaches, nausea, weight loss or gain, insomnia, high blood pressure, gastrointestinal disorders

- Losing the ability to concentrate at work or in school

- Experiencing stress in relationships with coworkers, friends, and family

As a result of sexual harassment women have forfeited research, work, and even careers. Women report having to avoid classes or working with certain instructors because they felt at risk for being subjected to sexual harassment. Many women change their majors or educational programs because of sexual harassment. Sometimes they simply drop out of college entirely. Too often a woman will blame herself for an incident and her self-esteem and self-confidence will suffer. She may experience physical symptoms, including gastrointestinal disorders and headaches. The effects may appear even after the victim drops out of a course, changes her major, or drops out of school. The victim's anger may not be easily expressed, so she suffers alone, experiencing feelings of helplessness, powerlessness, and increasing isolation. Sexual harassment can damage a woman's sense of competence and self-esteem.

CASE STUDIES OF SEXUAL HARASSMENT

The following case studies are included to give you a full appreciation of what sexual harassment is and it's damaging after-effects. All the examples included here are true-life incidents solicited from women from two sources—a small, northeastern college, and a large southeastern university. All the contributors wished to remain anonymous.

Example 1

Sexual harassment can have a powerful impact on women's selection of careers, according to a study published in 1982 by "The Project on the Status and Education of Women on the Association of American Colleges." In this first example, we see the impact of gender harassment upon a woman's academic choices.

> I am a white female, and when I was fifteen, a sophomore in high school, I took a geometry class with a white, male teacher who was in his late fifties. He was quite sexist, subtly, and often not so subtly. One of those not-so-subtle incidents occurred one day when addressing the class. He said, "I know all you girls are not interested in math like the boys are."

> It would be easy to write this off, saying that it wasn't that big of a deal, but I was really offended. He made other comments like, "Go home and cry to your mother," when I asked him to slow down a little and explain something.

> My mother wrote a letter to the principal, and as I recall, there was neither a reply, nor any real notice taken of the issue.

> In taking a Psychology of Women course in college, I've learned how girls are dissuaded at a very early age from persuing math and science. It makes me angry to think that this teacher may have had some influence in my decision to take only three years of math in high school, and probably only one semester in college, even though I was never that bad at math. If I could go back in time, I would probably take the situation more seriously, and consider all of the future students who would be influenced by such comments. I would want the community to be aware that their tax dollars are paying the salary of a man who is enforcing gender stereotyping and leaving many young girls with negative attitudes toward math.

Example 2

Derogatory comments about womens' bodies can have a long-lasting impact and lower self-esteem. In this example, a woman describes her encounters with a dance instructor whose sexist comments affected several women students.

I am a twenty-one year-old white woman, a senior at a small liberal arts college. My majors are American Studies and Gender Studies. The teacher described in this incident is a white man who is in his late forties or early fifties.

I have been taking dance in my college's drama/dance department since I was a freshman. I am currently enrolled in four dance classes, three of which are ballet. Three of my teachers use positive reinforcement to encourage the students. One, however, the man in his late forties, early fifties, takes cheap shots at students. One day he told me my arm looks like a noodle. This did not make me feel good about myself. It puts me on edge around him. Another day, he came over, put his arm around me, and said, "You've gained a little weight this summer."

I instantly felt self-conscious and insecure. On another occasion, he went over to a classmate of mine, a wonderful dancer with a beautiful body, put his hand on her stomach, and said, "This looks like blubber. There is no reason that anyone as skinny as you should have a stomach that looks like blubber."

She nodded her head in agreement, but it was apparent that she felt mortified.

This will be my last semester of dance. In December, I will be asked to complete an evaluation on this instructor. I plan to give him an unfavorable rating and write a letter to the dean, explaining these incidents and the detrimental effect they have had on the self-esteem of the women in his classes.

Example 3

Here's an example of self-blame resulting from coerced sexual relations.

I was very close to graduating with my bachelor's degree in social studies comprehensive when I was told by my advisor that I needed to take several courses in economics. These courses were very hard for me. I felt I would never graduate, and here I was, in my fifth year of college.

Then I met Clyde, professor of economics. I went to his office and told him about my predicament. He invited me to lunch. Afterwards, he asked if I wanted to see his apartment and meditate with him. At his apartment, he showed me several books on Zen meditation. Next thing I knew, he was kissing me.

During the next nine months of our affair, Clyde signed me up for several economics courses he was teaching, including a course called "Economics for Engineers." I had to laugh when he gave me a B in this class and other classes he taught, where I never even set foot in the classroom. Thanks to Clyde, I completed required courses and was able to graduate, but inside, I feel awful about what I did.

Example 4

According to a Hunter College pamphlet on sexual harassment entitled *Sexual Harassment on Campus is a Problem,* "Recent research revealed that out of 265 women graduate students surveyed, 21 percent reported that they had not enrolled in a course in order to avoid harassment, 11.3 percent had reported the harassment, 2.6 percent dropped a course because of harassment, and 15.9 percent were directly assaulted."

Here is an example of a woman changing her major and forfeiting her career goal of becoming a journalist because of sexual harassment.

On the first day of class, I walked in about ten minutes late and he stopped right in the middle of his lecture and began ogling me right in front of the class. "What nationality are you?" he asked. "Italian," I answered. "Oh, I have a thing for Italian women," he said.

It was my first semester as a graduate student in journalism. My undergraduate degree had been education and I wanted to switch vocations. The Dean of the College of Journalism said I'd have to backtrack a little and take a few basic journalism courses before I could be approved for graduate school, since my under-graduate degree had been in another field. It was imperative, he said, that I get A's or B's in these basic courses in order to get approved. To tell you the truth, I was glad the professor had "a thing for Italian women," for I felt uncertain about my abilities as a journalist. I thought, "He'll probably give me extra help." Well! He certainly wanted to give me more than extra in-class help!

After that first class, he invited me to have a drink with him at a local bar. I went, still unsuspecting. He described his horrible relationships with his four ex-wives and said that the alimony payments were killing him. He wanted to know if I'd join him for supper at a Chinese restaurant that Saturday. I initially said "yes," but on Saturday morning I called him with the "perfect excuse." After that I started avoiding him.

After that, everything I wrote seemed to be very wrong. I started receiving the lowest of low grades in the entire class. Yes, I'd initially been uncertain about my writing abilities, but I didn't think my writing was that horrible.

I began making appointments with the dean, who was about to retire. He sympathized with me and told me to keep bringing my writing to him every week. He personally felt that papers I was receiving F's on were examples of good, clear reporting. Unfortunately, he retired before the semester ended.

The professor gave me a D in the basic journalism class, the lowest grade. I went to see the new dean. It turned out he was good buddies with the professor in question. He said, "If you think you're that hot of a writer, take the class again with another professor."

Guess what? The other professor was also best friends with the professor in question. When I began receiving failing grades on all my papers, I knew it was no use. I dropped out of journalism.

However, with two semesters of journalism courses, I *did* manage to get a job as a reporter for a small southern newspaper.

Guess what? The editor was having an affair with the publisher. They broke up and he wanted me to step in her shoes—not just as editor, mind you. I went back to college and decided to pursue a master's in education.

Example 5

Many women change courses, drop out of courses, or "duck" to avoid a professor who has been harrassing them. Here is an example.

I was sexually harassed by my committee chairman (no longer my committee chairman). Physical and verbal advancements were made by the professor. I said nothing for fear of some punishment or consequence (grade, reputation, maybe told by my college it was my fault, etc.) This went on for six months.

Instead, I changed my phone number (so he couldn't call anymore) and never came to speak to him again. I removed him from my committee. I never took a class from him again (classes I needed to take I had to let go). I avoided him on campus, sometimes hiding behind cars and trees to avoid him.

After six months I confided my problem with a professor and I was encouraged to complain. I made a formal complaint to the Dean of Arts and Sciences. The professor was reprimanded but that's all. I later learned that he is a habitual offender and had previously been formally warned. The university has still done nothing to modify this "difficult teacher's" behavior inspite of even more recent complaints. No punishment and his behavior continues.

The way this problem should have been handled is that the first time I warned him not to touch me he should have respected me. That should have been enough. The second way the continued problem should have been handled is a firing or suspension of that teacher by the university in the face of his habitual offenses. Neither happened. Again, my main gripe with difficult teachers is when they take advantage of their powerful position to cause fear, hostility, intimidation, and embarrassment to a student. Of course, sexual harassment has all the facets of men over women, etc., but it really just boils down to power abusers.

In every case I've encountered with "difficult teachers," there is inevitably a personal problem with the teacher. The student must believe in himself/herself and not feel inadequate or stupid. I really thought this teacher believed in me as a good student. I need that encouragement. When I realized what he really wanted from me, I felt like, "I must not be a very good student after all." I've since recognized that he has the problem—not me.

Research indicates that most, if not all, sexual harassers are repeat offenders.

Example 6

Sexual harassment is a betrayal of trust. It often has incestuous-like overtones. This next example illustrates how a student experienced a serious betrayal of trust with a teacher she admired.

I had confided in a certain teacher many times about problems I was having with my parents. He was always very supportive, a good listener. I appreciated him so much. He was like a father to me, and I respected him, knowing he would not break a confidence.

One day, I entered his office, crying hysterically, as I reported yet another incident with my parents. He said, "Come here. Let me give you a hug."

Still crying hysterically, I felt relieved being held by this big, tall, father-like man. Suddenly, while I was still crying, he cupped my entire breast with his hand and quickly took his fingertips and squeezed my nipple. I hastily backed away, feeling shocked and horrified.

This was a father-like man I had trusted. I never confided in him again.

Example 7

Researchers Billie Wright Dziech and Linda Weiner, authors of *The Lecherous Professor* (1990), say that sexual harassment can shatter a woman's personal belief system. Here is an example of a value-shattering experience.

I remember as a little girl my mother explicitly telling me never to accept a ride or candy from a stranger. I remember that message repeatedly being told to me by teachers, by "Officer Friendly," and by other authority figures.

This message was deeply imbedded into my thought pattern— "Don't trust strangers." But no one ever suggested—not my parents, not teachers, not even members of the clergy—that teachers would ever do something harmful to me. On the contrary, I was taught to respect teachers, to emulate them, to look to them for guidance and knowledge. Not in my wildest imagination would I have ever dreamed that an invitation to dinner from a favorite teacher means he wants to sleep with me and will punish me if I don't. The idea simply did not exist in my mind. To me, teachers were grown-ups I could talk to who cared about me.

There was a teacher I really admired. He introduced me to Carl Jung's theories of depth psychology which really helped me to understand myself. He was so helpful. He was like a father to me. He was always willing to discuss depth psychology with me outside of class. I respected him. I emulated him.

One day, while visiting him in his office, he asked me to lunch. After lunch, we were back at his office. We had just arrived. He suddenly embraced me tightly, pressing an erection against me, and he kissed me. I was shocked! Before I could back away, as he was still holding me, he said, "It's quite clear that we've felt this way about each other for a long time."

I was thoroughly shocked. I pushed him away and displayed my bewilderment. After that, he was very cold and businesslike to me. Our intellectual discussions ceased. He no longer showed interest in me.

Example 8

Sexual harassment is not limited to college or high school incidents. According to Victor J. Ross and John Marlowe, authors of *The Forbidden Apple: Sex in the Schools* (1985), sexual harassment also occurs in grade school and in junior high. In fact, the authors report that incidents are on the increase. They suggest that students avoid situations where they are alone with a teacher, such as on the playground or after school.

In junior high school I had a history teacher who would give girls a hard time if they didn't wear dresses. Every time a girl wore a dress he would take a picture of her. Some fathers complained (mine was one of them). He then had to leave that school. When I got to high school I had the same teacher for sociology. He gave me a hard time the whole year. I got mono at the end of the year and missed quite a bit of school. He wouldn't give me my make-up work; my parents tried to get the make-up work. I ended up with a D in the class. We brought it to the attention of the administration. We were told that disciplinary action would be taken. I don't know if it was taken.

All he needed to do was give me my make-up work. What's so hard about that? To this day, I wonder if he was holding a grudge for what happened in junior high school.

Example 9

Sexual harassment doesn't always end with a bad grade. Sometimes the professor will give the student an undeserved high grade as a way of avoiding an official complaint.

It was near the end of the winter semester and my roomate, Ines, and I were both preparing to take our statistics final. Neither of us had done very well in the course. As roommates, we had often studied together, but we just could not understand most of the math formulae and terms.

The professor was a handsome man in his mid-thirties from Iran. Since Ines and I were the only females in his class, we used to sit up front, giggle, whisper about him, and fantasize that he was our sweetheart. As nineteen year-olds, we, of course, never expected this to happen nor did we want it to happen.

On the day of the final exam, both of us were worried that we might not pass the course. I sat there, during the exam, staring at a paper filled with numbers and formulas that looked as foreign to me as the Iranian language.

Before I was half-way finished with the test, the professor signaled for me to come up to his desk. I walked apprehensively, certain that his cue meant I was failing the course.

"What are you doing after this final?" he asked. I told him I had another final in English but after that I would be free. He asked if I would come to his office at that time and I said I would.

Following the English final, Ines went home and I went to Professor Rhonagy's office. I was certain he was going to tell me I had flunked the course.

As I made my way up the stairs to the Statistics Department, I could hear the sounds of professors laughing and wishing each other a Merry Christmas. Everyone seemed anxious to pack his belongings as quickly as possible and begin the two weeks' Christmas vacation.

Professor Rhonagy, also packing, greeted me enthusiastically. "Hello! Have you eaten your lunch yet?"

I said I hadn't because I had been so busy with finals. "Then, where would you like to go?" he asked. I felt embarrassed, surprised, and a little apprehensive—still wondering if this meant he was going to break the news over lunch that I had flunked. Hesitantly, I replied, "Anywhere is okay with me." "Fine," he said. "Then we shall go to the Brown Derby for steak."

We hurried downstairs and he opened the door to his yellow Volkswagen for me. All the way to the restaurant, he made pleasant, light conversation. He was always so friendly and personable.

At the restaurant, he ordered me a Josephine and for himself, a Napoleon. We sat in a dark, quiet corner sipping daquiris and eating hors d'oeuvres before our meals arrived. I expressed my philosophies on many deep subjects and he said I was very mature for nineteen.

As we enjoyed our steaks, the professor asked me what my plans were for the Christmas break. I told him that Ines and I were planning to take a bus to Chicago and stay with some friends. His eyes widened and he smiled vehemently as he announced, "Why, isn't that interesting? I just happen to be going to Chicago to visit my brother." The professor said there was no need for us to take a bus, that we could simply ride with him.

He drove me home and I asked Ines if she would rather go to Chicago with Professor Rhonagy than take a bus. He agreed to pick us up early the following morning.

When he arrived the next day, Ines and I greeted him with several bags of clothing, make-up, etc. We overpacked since we wouldn't be lugging things on and off of buses.

As we were loading up his car, he noticed my large, angora cat. "Who will take care of her?" he inquired. I told him we had a friend who hates cats who had reluctantly agreed to feed her in our absence. "Then, take the cat with us!" he declared. Soon we were on our way to Chicago with six bags of clothes, a litter box, and a cat.

It was ten hours to Chicago. To help pass the time, Ines brought a deck of playing cards. Bergie, the cat, slept on the back seat while Ines passed cards to the professor and me. The time passed quickly. By 2 A.M., we had reached the Chicago freeway.

"It's much too late to disturb your friends," Professor Rhonagy announced. "And, certainly, I don't want to disturb my brother at this hour. So, I suggest we stay in a motel." Ines and I turned simultaneously and gave each other a curious look. "No hanky-panky," he quickly added.

Ines shrugged but looked a little concerned. I nodded. Pulling into a Travelodge, Professor Rhonagy suggested we stay in the car so he could get a cheaper rate.

It was a very cold night in Chicago, so cold you could see your breath inside the motel room. The cat sniffed around all the corners and then curled up by the T.V. There was only one double bed in the room, so Professor Rhonagy suggested that Ines and I sleep in the bed and he would sleep on the floor, using a spare blanket and pillow.

Sometime, during the middle of the night, I heard Professor Rhonagy talking to himself, complaining about the cold. Next thing I know, he had joined us in the bed, with me in the middle. "Oh, he won't try anything," I remember thinking. "He's my professor!"

About a half hour later, I woke up with his hand on my breast and his groins pressed against my behind. I awoke Ines and we moved onto the floor.

"What's the problem?!" Professor Rhonagy asked seemingly innocent. We refused to answer him. Angered, he said, "You're acting very immature. Come back into the bed and I'll go back onto the floor."

In the morning, I was awoken by a persistent light tapping upon my left shoulder. I looked up. It was Professor Rhonagy, fully dressed, his briefcase in his left hand, hat on his head, wearing his trenchcoat. "I'm leaving now," he announced in a very cold, business-like voice. "It's eleven o'clock. Check-out time is in one hour." And he left. Just like that.

Stranded in the middle of Chicago, with little money, several bags, and a cat, we did manage to locate our friends who were surprised by this unbelievable story. They loaned us enough money to take a bus back to our hometown at the end of our vacation. Prior to leaving, however, they called Professor Rhonagy. "We have a couple of girls here who say they were supposed to catch a ride back to Ohio with you," said one.

"I have no idea what you're talking about," said Professor Rhonagy. "I haven't been to Chicago in years." And he hung up.

When we arrived back home our report cards were awaiting us in the mailbox. We expected to receive failing grades. To our surprise, Ines received a B, and I, an A. Apparently, Professor Rhonagy didn't want any complaints of sexual harassment lodged against him.

Example 10

Sexual harassment happens more frequently to graduate students than to undergraduate students. About thirty percent of graduate women can expect to be harassed. Often, the effects of sexual harassment are so traumatizing that the graduate blocks out the memories for years to come.

According to psychologist Sandra Shullman, traumatic experiences like sexual harassment are frequently repressed. Victims may remember the experience in bits and pieces or lose chronological order, but the "descriptions of harassment may become clearer over time as the mind retrieves more memories" (Women's Legal Defense Fund 1991).

Sexual harassment in U.S. colleges and universities is a major barrier to women's professional development and a traumatic force that disrupts and damages their personal lives (Betz and Fitzgerald 1987).

It's been nine years since I graduated with the Ph.D. I've never used the Ph.D.; that is, I've never held a job as a professor in higher education. It's only been within the last year that I've been able to clearly articulate what happened to me and describe the traumatic impact it had upon my life, my self-concept, and my career.

In the summer of 1980, my chairman asked me to take a graduate level class with a colleague and friend of his, Dr. Binger. Dr. Binger was up for tenure and promotion but had not published enough research. The purpose of the course was to have graduate students help Dr. Binger generate research ideas. Mind you, the true purpose of the course was never overtly spoken. But it became quite clear in our minds, within a few weeks of the class, that we were being used to generate research ideas for a professor whose job was on the line.

This was the most ridiculous class I have ever taken. At break times, the students would whisper to one another and snicker about the absurdity of the class. In class, however, everyone tried to appear interested so they wouldn't get on Dr. Binger's bad side. Everyone, that is, except me. I sat in class looking obviously bored. Sometimes I rolled my eyes. To give you an idea of the absurdity of this class, let me share with you some of the things we discussed. "Man literally lives within his skin." "Objects farther away look smaller than objects close by." "When you're in a room, you not only perceive the room but yourself in the room." I'm not kidding and I'm not exaggerating when I tell you this. The professor would stand on a chair and proclaim with great enthusiasm, "Man literally lives in his skin. But how do we know that for sure? How can we prove that statement scientifically?"

One day, Dr. Binger asked us if we had experienced any "environmental perceptions" over the weekend, and one student replied, "Yes! I was watching pigeons walk across a telephone wire, and I noted how they bob their heads back and forth, and I wondered if the bobbing affects how they perceive the world." I had to bite my lip to keep from laughing. The professor said, "Very good! Very good! But how can we research that concept?"

A student placed a can of Tab soda on top of his papers so the breeze from an open window wouldn't blow them away. The professor said, "You're using this can of Tab soda as a paperweight! How did you know to do that? How can we prove that scientifically?" It was bizarre.

Noticing my obvious lack of enthusiasm for his class, the professor stopped me at the end of the period one day and asked me my honest opinion of the class. Thinking he wanted my honest opinion, I gave it to him. "I think it's the most ridiculous class I've ever taken. And everybody else in here pretty much feels the same way."

Dr. Binger started acting very coldly toward me after that. I told my chairman about the course and said, "If he gives me a vendetta grade, I'm going to write an article for the campus paper about this ridiculous class." My chairman didn't believe me. He said, "Oh, you wouldn't do that."

I didn't realize that the publishing of that letter in the campus newspaper would be a turning point in my life. I was raised to believe that we all have First Amendment rights, here in the

United States of America, and that part of our First Amendment rights include freedom to voice dissenting opinions. The course was lousy and ridiculous; I voiced my opinion in a letter to the editor, and, as a result, I was blackballed by my department. My chairman resigned. I approached everyone in the department and asked if they would chair me. Everyone treated me as if I were a pariah.

Many students would have terminated their studies at that point. But no, I was determined. As I saw it, I'd already completed twelve long, hard, and expensive years of college. I wanted and I felt I deserved to obtain a Ph.D.

One sympathetic professor, to whom I told my dilemma, suggested I lie low, take extra courses (courses I didn't need), and show the professors in my department that I'd changed. "You're going to have to learn how to conform," he said.

About a year after I had turned into a quiet, noncontroversial, conforming individual, I took a class with Jordan. Jordan, freshly divorced, had just terminated an intimate relationship with another graduate student. He said, "I'll chair you under one condition—that I hand-select your entire committee." You guessed it—he appointed my former chairman and his other personal buddies to serve on my committee.

It soon became obvious that Jordan had other expectations of me besides selecting my committee. He began inviting me to lunch. And then to dinner. We attended parties together. I played racquetball and tennis with him. He took me to fancy steak houses for supper. One day he invited me to go to a historical museum with him after lunch. We walked through the museum arm in arm, hand in hand, like two lovers.

I was afraid to turn him down for these dates. I was afraid he would stop chairing me. He knew he had me over a barrel. No one else wanted to chair me, so without him, I couldn't obtain a Ph.D. So, I went along. I smiled. I listened to all of his stories about what a wonderful lover he was. But I was always able to come up with a legitimate excuse to get out of sleeping with him.

After about a year of lunch dates, dinner dates, etc., and I had still not slept with Jordan, he invited me to attend an out-of-town conference with him. Once again, I felt obligated to comply.

"Don't worry about paying for your own hotel room," he said. "There is a spare bed in my room." I always had the "perfect" excuse. "Oh, Jordan, how sweet of you, but I just happen to have a friend in that town and I already promised her I would stay with her. She would be very disappointed if I didn't."

The conference—and my not sharing a hotel room with Jordan—was a real turning point in our relationship. After we returned from the conference, Jordan became noticeably cold and distant toward me. He had "courted" me for almost a year—dinner dates, lunch dates, private parties, racquetball, tennis, visits to the museum, etc. After the conference it finally became very obvious to Jordan that I had no intention of sleeping with him. He stopped inviting me to lunch, etc. And that's when the vendetta began.

The Vendetta—Qualifying Exams

It was the day before my qualifying exams. Jordan said I would be taking the exam in a vacationing professor's office. I asked him if I could type, rather than write by hand, my responses. I told him I could bring my own IBM Selectric typewriter. Jordan agreed, saying, "But you'll have to bring your typewriter the day before the qualifying exams begin so you can start the exams promptly at 8 A.M."

On the day before the exams, around 4 P.M., I arrived at the college with my typewriter. The vacationing professor's office was locked. The secretaries had no key to his office. Where was I supposed to take the exams? No other private place had been arranged for me. With heavy typewriter in hands, I walked to Jordan's office and told him I had something very serious to discuss with him. He just happened to be in the middle of interviewing a new woman graduate student who wanted Jordan to chair her. Disinterested in me and my dilemma, Jordan said, "Can't you see I'm busy with this student?! You'll have to wait out in the hall until we're through."

An hour and a half later, I was still standing in the hall with my typewriter. Jordan and the new student were in his office, laughing, joking, and making light conversation. I peeked into his office. "Jordan, this is a very serious matter. I'm scheduled to take the qualifying exams tomorrow."

"Don't ever interrupt me ever again," he snapped. Jordan did resolve the matter. Then he took me inside his office and made an ominous threat. "You're getting ready to take your qualifying exams tomorrow," he began. "If you pass them, that means we begin the very long journey of doing your dissertation. If I'm going to remain your chairman, you must do as I say from here on out. If you ever interrupt me or do anything to irritate me from this point on, I plan to resign as your chairman. Would you like me to do that?"

Shocked, I didn't reply.

He repeated, "I said, would you like me to resign as your chairman? I can do that right now." And he stood up and walked toward his door.

"No, no, Jordan. I don't see any big problem here," I said. I knew he was really angry because I had not started a romantic relationship with him. It was so obvious.

Jordan continued. "You know, the only reason I agreed to chair you up until now is because I was on an Eastern religion kick. I'm over that now and there's no need for me to chair you."

We both knew that he was the only one in the department even remotely willing to chair me. "I promise I'll comply," I said.

Vendetta Incident 2

I scheduled an appointment to review a chapter of my dissertation with Jordan. He failed to show up for the appointment. I left several messages for him to call me over the next several days. None of my calls were returned. Finally, I reached Jordan. "Oh, I forgot," he said. "We'll just have to reschedule, won't we?" This incident happened at least half a dozen times.

I started to feel the "message" I was getting—Jordan was indirectly telling me to go away. He no longer had a use for me. He had found a new graduate student.

Vendetta Incident 3

This third incident became a recurrent transaction between Jordan and me, becoming somewhat of a ritual. I would go to Jordan's office so he could critique my dissertation. He'd quickly scan it and say, "This chapter is not right. It needs to be redone."

"What's wrong with it the way it is?" I'd ask. He'd snap, "I can't spoon-feed you for the rest of your life. Look at other dissertations in the library and figure it out."

At first I would mildly protest. "I'm not about to change it unless I know what is specifically the problem. I don't see any problem here."

Jordan would repeat his threat of resigning as my chairman. "Do you want me to resign right now? I can do that," he would remind me. And he'd extend his arm and point with his index finger to the office.

Thereafter, if I voiced the most minor objection, he'd simply point to the office. This pointing ritual—the pointed finger with the extended arm—represented his awesome power over me. A deep well of rage was beginning to fester inside of me. The longer the ritual continued, the more deeply I felt the rage, I learned to smile, bite my tongue, and tell Jordan I would make the necessary corrections.

I really did want an honest, straight-forward, detailed critique. But all I got was vague, apathetic feedback such as, "You know what needs to be done." When the lunch dates were occuring, he used to tell me I was the best, the brightest. Now, I felt myself losing confidence in my academic abilities. How was I supposed to judge the quality of high level academic work I'd never done before?

Vendetta Incident 4

B.H., a marginal graduate student from Saudi Arabia, started his Ph.D. program two years later than I did. He was graduating, while I was still, at Jordan's request, writing and rewriting my dissertation. Jordan, at one time, had asked me to tutor B.H., to help prepare him for the qualifying exams because his comprehension of the subject matter—and English in general—was very poor. How was it that this marginal student, who had been tutored by me, was graduating while I was still plugging away?

The nonverbal message Jordan was giving was quite obvious to me: Jordan hoped, through attrition, that I would leave and terminate my program. Would Jordan finally allow me to graduate? Or would I eventually drop out and go away? These disturbing, anxiety-producing questions began running though my mind obsessively.

Vendetta Incident 5

Its years later, and I still haven't graduated. And I haven't gone away. There's a big case of sexual harassment going on in a department closely affiliated with my department. It turns out the professor in question has slept with dozens of women graduate students from the department. One got pregnant and had an abortion. When she filed an official complaint, several of the other women came forward to tell their stories. None of them knew about the others.

Suddenly, Jordan and the other members of my committe have decided it's time for me to graduate. I was relieved, thinking I'll finally get a decent job in higher education. But now, Jordan throws me a new curve ball, telling me, "I won't be able to give you any kind of job reference after you graduate unless you spend an extra year rewriting your dissertation and turning it into a publishable piece with my name as senior author."

A male student of Jordan's had recently graduated and had obtained a good job at the University of Alabama. He had not remained an extra year rewriting his dissertation, turning it into a publishable piece. Jordan had found him a job.

Vendetta Incident 6

It was finally my graduation day. At the ceremony, all the other graduating Ph.D.s had their chairmen escorting them down the aisle and across the stage as they received their diplomas in front of thousands of witnesses—all of them except for me. Unescorted, I felt cheap and unimportant. I didn't really feel like I had graduated.

The next day I asked Jordan why he hadn't shown up. "I didn't know you were going to attend," he replied, even though I had clearly told him I would be attending my graduation ceremony.

End of the Vendetta—Or is There an End to This Vendetta?

I saw an attorney shortly after graduation and described the nightmare that had occurred. "Too bad you didn't sleep with him," he said. "We would have a stronger case."

I visited the campus Affirmative Action counselor and described the situation to her. She said, "Well, now that it's over, just go ahead and apply for jobs and just don't tell anybody about it."

Jordan was never reprimanded in any way. Jordan wrote me a letter stating that he could never recommend me for a job because I hadn't turned my dissertation into a publishable piece. Without a recommendation from a chairman, it's very difficult, if not impossible, to obtain a job in higher education—especially since there's a scarcity of jobs anyway.

When the sexual harassment began, years ago, I became very nervous all the time. I saw a doctor because I started suffering from severe migraine headaches. I gained weight and developed black circles under my eyes.

After I finally graduated, I became emotionally paralyzed. My confidence and my beliefs had been shattered. I couldn't act or think. There was such a large discrepancy in my mind between how I was raised to view teachers and all that had happened to me. It took years to piece it altogether in my mind and make sense of it.

I wanted to admire Jordon, to emulate him, but how could I? When I entered graduate school, my goals were to help students, to be a great, inspiring teacher, and to publish meaningful research. When I graduated, I thought, "How could one accomplish noble objectives within a system that gives license to violate innocent students?"

I entered higher education an innocent. I believed professors were highly knowledgeable, caring human beings that one listens to, respects, and obeys. I left feeling that only the most selfish, self-centered, self-absorbed, and self-serving individuals survive academic careers.

WHAT YOU CAN DO ABOUT SEXUAL HARASSMENT

There are four ways you can deal with sexual harassment:

1. Individual recourse

2. Institutional recourse

3. Federal recourse

4. Legal recourse

INDIVIDUAL REMEDIES

Most sexual harassment starts off at a very mild level (sexual innuendoes, sexist comments, "jokes"). Many women ignore the early stages of sexual harassment or convince themselves that it didn't really happen.

According to a report in the *New York Times* (11 March, 1992), "Most of the girls said they were troubled by the boys' behavior but felt helpless to respond. 'It might be so bad you want to ignore it,' said one eighth grader. 'It might be you don't know what to do so you act like it never happened.'" This only worsens the situation. The following suggestions are designed to prevent sexual harassment at its onset and prevent it from escalating.

1. Recognize the early stages of sexual harassment.

2. Do not ignore it. Silence makes it worse.

3. Assert yourself. Verbally confront the harasser.

4. Keep a record.

5. Tell others what has happened to you.

6. Send the harasser a letter.

7. Do not give mixed messages.

    a. Be friendly, not familiar.

    b. Maintain a professional appearance.

    c. Do not accept social invitations of any kind.

    d. Avoid spending time alone in the professor's office, if possible.

Recognize the early stages of sexual harassment. Early stages of sexual harassment include:

- Sexual gazing.

- Jokes, innuendos, derogatory comments about women in general.

- Winks and other flirtatious behavior that is unwanted, unwelcome, and not returned.

- Talk of a sexualized nature, such as asking you about your love life or telling you about his, and comments about your appearance.

Women have been conditioned to view these behaviors as "innocent."

Most ignore it. However, comments, gazing, and other behaviors listed above are ways that harassers lay the foundation for future harassment.

Do not ignore it. Silence makes it worse. Since sexual harassment, by definition, is unwanted sexual attention, the harasser needs to know, right from the start, that his comments are not wanted. Otherwise, he will misinterpret the silence as approval or mutual interest, and the harassment will continue.

Assert yourself. Verbally confront the harasser. Here are ways to respond to the five early stages of sexual harassment:

Student: Sir, I have a great idea for our research proposal!

Professor: Well! If your idea is as good as you look in that sweater, I'll certainly go for it!

Student: (Doesn't ignore it, immediately confronts in a diplomatic manner.) Sir, my purpose in being here today is to discuss an idea I have for a research proposal. I don't believe my appearance has any bearing on that, but thanks for the compliment. Now, as I was saying, here is an outline I have for our research proposal. In point number one, I suggest . . .

Bravo for the student in this example! She (1) stated the purpose for the meeting, (2) acknowledged his comment in a way that showed respect for the professor but will discourage further comments, and (3) got right back on track. This student managed to maintain professional talk with a professor who might be inclined to become overly-familiar and harass his students.

Sexual gazing

A professor has asked the student to reshelve books that require her to use a ladder. While she reshelves the books, the professor lies prone on the floor and looks up her skirt! (When this happened in real life, the student was so embarrassed that she remained silent and continued to reshelve the books.)

How can a student handle the situation illustrated above? Immediately descend the ladder and say, "Sir, I really don't have time to reshelve your books. I see that you're lying on the floor. If you're not feeling well, I suggest that you go to the infirmary." Then exit.

Unless the professor is completely dense, he will understand that the student did not approve of his unprofessional behavior. By gently confronting and immediately leaving, the student is less likely to experience future incidents of sexual harassment than one who would stay and comply.

Responding to jokes, innuendoes, or derogatory comments about women in general. Many women, out of embarrassment, laugh when a man tells a joke that portrays women as sexual objects. But the laughter serves to encourage the harasser. A student who must listen to such "jokes" and comments can get the conversation back on track.

Professor: And let me tell you the latest blonde joke.

Student: (interrupting) Sir, I'm here to review this paper. Here are the results I have so far.

Notice how the student states her purpose for the meeting. She (1) shows respect for the professor as a professional, and (2) keeps the conversation flowing in a professional direction.

Handling winks and other inappropriate flirtatious behavior. An overly-polite student will feel extremely uncomfortable when a professor winks or gestures at her in a flirtatious manner. She may smile, uncomfortably, not knowing what to do. The smile, however, only tends to encourage the harasser to continue his behavior.

Instead of smiling, the student needs to explicitly express her uncomfortable feelings. This can be done using a technique called *The Three-Part Assertive Message.*

1. Describe the offending behavior as objectively as possible. "When you . . ."

2. Explain how you feel. "I feel . . ."

3. Tell what you want in the future. "I would appreciate it if . . ."

A three-part assertive message might sound like this: "Sir, when you wink at me, I feel extremely uncomfortable. I respect you as a professional and I want to keep our relationship on a professional level."

The purpose of the three-part assertive message is to openly explain to the harasser what is offending you, how you feel, and what you want. It works much more effectively than smiling out of embarrassment or saying nothing.

Handling talk of a sexualized nature. Sometimes sexual harassment begins with a teacher who talks to a student on a too-familiar basis, such as asking about your love life, or telling you about his.

Professor: My wife—I love her—but we don't have a very good love life.

Student: (interrupting) Sir, we're here today to work on the data of this project. May I suggest we reschedule this appointment? Is tomorrow at 3 o'clock a good time for you, or would you prefer tomorrow at 4 o'clock to discuss these data?

Bravo for this student! She (1) stated the purpose of the meeting, and (2) suggested alternative times to discuss the data. The professor will strongly get the message that his talk was inappropriate and he will be much less inclined to carry on a sexualized conversation with the student in the future. This will work much better than a student who quietly listens, out of embarrassment, to a professor who drones on about his unsatisfying love life.

In all of the above examples, the student gave no reinforcement to inappropriate behavior. Silent treatment, smiling, and engaging in casual talk—encourage harassers to continue what they are doing. Behavior modification is much more effective than waging hostile threats to a harasser. ("I'm going to report you to authorities.") Remember: teachers are powerful people. Our goal is to gently redirect inappropriate behavior of a powerful person without alienating him.

If the harassment persists, start keeping a journal. If the harasser continues his behavior, it's very important to begin documenting each event, your reaction to the event, and who you told about the event. A journal strengthens your case if you decide to go to court years later. It cancels the potential objection that you've distorted the facts in your mind.

Dr. Richard Barickman, professor of English, Hunter College, said, "It's important to write down incidents, emotional reactions, physical symptoms, people you've talked to—anything that relates to it. Reporting the incidents to a sexual harassment panel can be very traumatic. The first act of reporting is reporting to yourself what happened. It's therapeutic for the victim."

The events should be written in a bound book where you cannot take out pages without it being noticed. This journal helps to uncover the secretive nature of sexual harassment.

Tell others about what has happened to you. There are two reasons why it is important to tell others what has happened to you: (1) It corroborates your story and provides you with a witness, and (2) it gives you a chance for a catharsis. When a person has experienced an upsetting event, it is important to tell that event to others as a way of releasing the hurt feelings. Dr. Barickman adds, "Telling others is also a type of reliving of the event. When reporting the harassment, you may want to bring a friend with you to (1) make you more comfortable, (2) serve as a witness to the reporting itself, (3) serve as a "reality check." Ask your friend later, 'Was I too upset?' (Barrickman 1992).

Send the harasser a letter. You've verbally confronted the harasser, but the harassment has continued. What can you do next? One of your options is to write the offender a letter, according to Mary Rowe, special assistant to the president of Massachusetts Institute of Technology (1981). Ms. Rowe recommends that the letter contain three parts.

Part I: State the facts. What happened? Where did it happen? What was said? What did the harasser do? When did it happen? (Include dates and times.) Who else witnessed the events, if anyone? State Prosecuting Attorney Rod Smith suggests that you include a statement, such as "My complaints include, but are in no way limited to, these specific examples." Otherwise, if you decided to go to court, the case might be limited to only the contents of the letter.

Part II: Describe (1) How you feel, and (2) your opinions (the damage you believe you've experienced). Examples of what might be included: "You have caused me to ask for a transfer to another class." "I am deeply embarrassed and worried that my parents will hear about this." "I am dropping out of the training course." "I feel terrible about what you did."

Part III: Tell what you want. Examples: "I want a chance to go over my work with you again and to reconsider my evaluation (grade)." Someone who feels she contributed to the problem might say, "Although we once were happily dating, it is important to me that we now reestablish a formal and professional relationship, and I ask you to do so."

Benefits of Writing a Letter

Most victims don't want to go to court, according to Ms. Rowe. They simply want the harassment to cease. The letter is not a panacea but, as a defense tactic, it is useful for several reasons.

- You have a written account of what happened. This account will become part of your evidence if you decide to appear before a sexual harassment or grievance panel, or if you decide to go to court.

- You'll feel like you did your best in getting the harassment to cease.

- Some harassers don't realize how their behavior is affecting the victim. The letter shows them concretely that their words and/or actions were unwelcome, unwanted, hurtful, or stressful.

- Many victims, embarrassed, don't want anyone else to know what happened to them. They also don't want to see the harasser get in any kind of trouble. The letter may get the harassment stopped without provoking publicity.

- Letter writing is a pro-active response. The victim starts to feel more of a sense of control over the situation. "Harassed people want to keep more control," said Ms. Rowe.

Disadvantages of Letter Writing

There are some disadvantages to writing a letter.

- According to research, harassers have generally victimized more than one person. A private letter does not encourage other victims to come forward and report their experiences.

- The institution will not be able to reprimand the harasser.

How to Send the Letter

If you decide that the advantages outweigh the disadvantages, you should implement one of the following procedures on the day you send the letter.

- Either deliver the letter in person to the harasser, and take a witness along who could later testify that he or she saw you hand the letter to the harasser.

- Send the letter through registered mail.

Don't send the letter to other persons, such as department heads, the chairman, or other personnel. Keep the tone of the letter factual and friendly and let the harasser know it is confidential correspondence. You may want to write on the envelope, "Personal and Confidential." That way, the harasser cannot later claim that you were trying to ruin his career.

Of course, keep a copy of the letter for yourself, for two reasons: (1) You may need it for court or grievance procedures; (2) "It may make you feel good about yourself for years," Ms. Rowe said.

Do not encourage being misread. Be friendly, not familiar. In a study of gender differences, researcher Antonia Abbey (1982), Northwestern University, discovered that " . . . men mistakenly interpret women's friendliness as an indication of sexual interest."

"Be friendly but business-like," recommends Ms. Lucille Rhim, Chairperson of a Commission on the Status of Women, City of Gainesville. "Overly-friendly means that you open up and talk about yourself personally. It can be misconstrued by the other person."

Maintain professional appearance.

"My daughters and I have had several disagreements about this subject," said Ms. Rhim. "'We should be able to wear whatever we want,' they say. It's true. But your appearance is a statement. Just like when you put on a business suit, it makes a statement. A woman has a right to wear whatever she wants to wear but assumptions can be made by the professor based upon her appearance."

Do not accept social invitations of any kind.

"If you start to accept dates where the two of you are alone he will again make assumptions. A professor may try to cross the boundaries, so the student must place a distinct boundary between herself and the professor. It is more difficult to maintain that boundary if she accepts the invitations," Ms. Rhim said.

Avoid spending time alone in the professor's office, if possible.

"Avoid time alone in his office. If you're spending a lot of time in his office, he can misinterpret and will see an emotional void and may take advantage."

These suggestions are in no way designed to blame the victim if she is sexually harassed. However, to avoid being misinterpreted or misread by members of the opposite sex in our culture, it is recommended that women students maintain professional appearance and conduct.

INSTITUTIONAL RECOURSE

So you've told the harasser to stop. You gave him both verbal and written notification. But the harassment continues. What can you do next? There are institutional remedies available on both the high school and college levels.

First, we will discuss grievance procedures on the college level.

THE SEXUAL HARASSMENT PANEL

Some progressive colleges have established sexual harassment panels specifically designed to meet students' needs. One university at the forefront is Hunter College in New York. The panel, established in 1982, is unusual because it is composed of faculty members, students, and staff from many departments. Dr. Richard Barickman, English Department, Hunter College, explained,

> The best reporting mechanism is a panel especially established just for sexual harassment. Why? Because women are reluctant to trust the power structure. If the dean is a friend of the professor, they don't trust reporting. There is a great uncertainty about the resources available and they don't know how to label what happened to them. Many blame themselves. They say, 'Did I say something to bring this upon myself?' So, our first step is to get them to feel comfortable enough to talk. Our panel is unusual. It's unusual to have a panel that's not part of a particular office and that is composed of students, faculty, and staff. Most universities have an affirmative action person. Other universities are following our example.

Hunter College also provides four-part workshops on sexual harassment for students, faculty, administrators, and staff.

> Yet education, however successful, is not sufficient in itself to prevent sexual harassment or to offer a recourse when it occurs. Because sexual harassment occurs in this context of institutional power, individuals who have been victimized are often, understandably, reluctant to use the ordinary channels in the college or university for resolving complaints. This is especially true because of the humiliating and disorienting impact of sexual harassment, where the victim may experience the sort of self-doubt, self-blame, and sense of degradation common to victims of rape, incest, and battering. It is important, therefore, that the means of hearing and resolving complaints of sexual harassment should be distinct from the regular departmental and administrative hierarchies.

> The fact that the panel at Hunter guarantees that all procedures will be confidential, and further guarantees that the individual

bringing the complaint can decide whether or not to make a formal complaint, encourages individuals to contact panel members to discuss a problem. Unless people—faculty, staff, and students—feel that they will have these protections, they will seldom report the sexual harassment they have experienced. Research findings fully support this conclusion. Obviously, individual complaints cannot be resolved nor can the pervasive injury done to the college community by sexual harassment be remedied, unless complaints are actually reported (Paludi and Barickman 1992).

The panel at Hunter College accepts both formal and informal complaints. Informal complaints have informal resolutions. For example, the professor may be asked to cease making sexist remarks in the classroom. Often, too, informal discussions with a panel member enable the person to deal with the problem on his or her own, or lead to an informal resolution through the assistance of members of the panel.

In the formal procedure, the victim writes a statement detailing her complaint. Three subcommittee members from the panel are selected to investigate. Both the victim and the accused appear before the subcommittee. They can bring witnesses and council, if they want. After the investigation is completed,

> ... we may recommend disciplinary action, or we may dismiss. Most of the time there is enough supportive evidence. In our experience, we find that the complaint has credibility. We then make recommendations for corrective actions—change of grade, transfer of employee, letter of reprimand, notice to department head, or even dismissal or loss of tenure (Paludi and Barickman 1992).

Universities that Just Don't Seem to Care

Not all universities are as dedicated as Hunter College in their quest to end sexual harassment on campus. Some universities give the impression that they're more concerned with making sure they are not sued for sexual harassment than preventing the emotional trauma and aftereffects that women who have been harassed typically experience.

I spoke to an administrator at a large, southeastern university about sexual harassment policies and procedures on his campus. Two years ago, a committee was formed to rewrite a university pamphlet on sexual harassment. After the pamphlet was printed, the committee was dissolved.

The pamphlet tells students who they can contact if they feel they've been sexually harassed. The list of contact persons includes deans, chairpersons, the affirmative action representative, other professors, or anyone in administration.

While the pamphlet was being written, the administration held workshops on sexual harassment for faculty, staff, and administration. They were told that sexual harassment must be reported. "There is no such thing as informal and formal complaint procedures on our campus," the administrator said. "All complaints of sexual harassment are treated in a formal manner. All complaints, whether written or oral, are reviewed."

At the time of review, the victim and the accused can bring witnesses and counsel. "We're talking about a professor's career. Sexual harassment is a serious charge. Of course, the accused has just as much right to tell his or her side of the story," he said.

The administrator explained that if a student wants the complaint to remain confidential, he or she can see a counselor on campus. Other than counselors, all others must report even the rumors they have heard. "We don't want a student coming back two years from now saying, 'I told you about this two years ago and you did nothing. Now I can sue for negligence.'"

I spent an afternoon tracking down the pamphlet on sexual harassment the disassembled committee had formulated. Calling several university offices, I was told, "We used to have the pamphet, but we seem to be out of them right now." Each department I called that didn't have the pamphlet—the provost office, student affairs, the library—suggested I call the counseling center. At the counseling center, a pleasant-sounding secretary suggested that I contact an off-campus crisis counseling center. Confused, I called the crisis center and said, "Are you part of the university?"

"No."

"Would you happen to have their pamphlet on sexual harassment?"

"No. Call their counseling center. They would have it."

"They told me to call you."

I next called an office on the campus for Sexual Assault and Recovery Services. The secretary said there was one copy in the office, so she couldn't mail it to me, but she'd try to track down another copy and send it to me. A week later, I received a photocopied article in the mail, an article on peer harassment—not teacher to student sexual harassment—with a note attached "I hope this helps with your research."

Finally, a librarian from this large university called me back. She said she had located the old sexual harassment pamphlet in a file folder, and that another staff member was willing to lend me her personal copy of the updated sexual harassment pamphlet. "I'll leave it in an envelope at the reference desk for you if you promise to return it," she said.

In the end, I contacted personnel and they actually had a copy of the pamphlet and agreed to mail it to me. I shared my adventure with the librarian who called back. "Yes. I often wonder what they would actually do if someone actually said, 'I've been sexually harassed,' " she said.

Here is an example of a student who felt her institution did not care. These are direct passages from an article that appeared in the *Gainesville Sun*, on Thursday, April 2:

UF Grad Student Claims Sexual Harassment

A highly regarded University of Florida graduate student has decided to go public with a sexual-harassment complaint against a research professor because she believes the university has taken too little action.

Sarah L. Freyer, 28, who came to Gainesville from Sarasota, has alleged that because of an untenable working situation with her mentor, Harmut Derendorf, a College of Pharmacy research professor, who was forced to leave the university and jeopardize a $66,000 grant from NASA.

"I am very dedicated to seeing this through. The pursuit of my career has been destroyed," Freyer told the *Sun*.

Derendorf, chairman of the department of pharmaceutics in the College of Pharmacy, said Wednesday that he is aware of the complaint. He said there is no validity to it.

"I stand behind my story and stand by my accusations 100 percent," Freyer said Wednesday. She also has lodged a complaint with the U.S. Equal Employment Opportunity Commission in Miami. At this point, she has chosen not to detail any allegations to the *Sun*.

In a Feb. 27 letter from UF assistant general counsel Barbara Wingo to Freyer's attorney, David Wagner obtained by the *Sun*, Wingo wrote that "the university is already in the process of investigating Freyer's complaint." Wingo added that information about the complaint from Freyer has been scant, and that has made it difficult for the university to proceed.

But Freyer says the university's system for dealing with these kinds of complaints is a shambles. For example, she cannot determine whether the university is treating her as an employee or a student. Freyer was both, but there are different routines for handling complaints from each.

"Our feeling is, we have been through all the university handbooks and guides, and there is no specific procedure for students to go through," Freyer said.

Catherine Longstreth, UF's associate vice president for academic affairs, said the university could do a better job of making people aware of procedures. She said the employee union is one avenue for complaints and the university has set out procedures, although they may not be well-known or easy to follow.

Longstreth has been conducting workshops on the UF campus to help communication. "There is a need to get these complaints in the right pew," she said.

Longstreth feared that the publicity on this case will discourage other people from coming forward with sexual-harassment complaints. The *Sun* has proceeded with Freyer's consent, however.

Longstreth also said the university is doing a much better job of keeping complainants informed of their cases, and when action is taken complainants are informed.

"We were bad about this years ago," she said.

Freyer first lodged her complaint in the College of Pharmacy in January with Dean Michael Schwartz. Subsequently, the investigation was removed "entirely from the purview of the College of Pharmacy" due to Freyer's concern that it already had been mishandled. "Nobody told me what my rights were," she said.

Freyer said she wanted the complaint investigated by Madelyn Lockhart, dean of the Graduate School. Lockhart had written a tough report on the way graduate students are treated by faculty at the college following the 1989 suicide of a graduate student.

Instead, the Office of Academic Affairs apparently is handling the complaint. Lockhart, though unable to talk about a specific complaint, said she could do the invesitgation under university rules. "I hear quite a few cases from time to time," Lockhart said.

Freyer is an honors student who received a UF presidential scholarship, a College of Pharmacy scholarship and an Upjohn Award for Excellence in Research. She was the first student to pursue her doctorate under a new doctoral program in the College of Pharmacy. She's been at the college for four years.

"I have strong standing . . . and I was an excellent student in the college," Freyer said. "If not, I don't think I would have courage to pursue it at all."

Freyer and Derendorf landed the NASA grant three years ago, and it paid the university $22,000 a year. She said the university is still paying her from that grant, although she has left. She's now working at a drugstore in High Springs.

DEPARTMENTAL RECOURSE

If you feel your sexual harassment complaint will fall upon deaf ears at the university, you can contact the U.S. Department of Education. There are ten regional offices across the United States in Boston, New York, Philadelphia, Atlanta, Chicago, Dallas, Kansas City (Missouri), Denver, San Francisco, and Seattle. Send a written complaint. An investigation will be conducted. The branch office will send the university a report concerning its findings. Recommendations to remedy the situation are suggested in a report by the committee. In extreme cases, the university may lose federal funding. The college or university is then periodically monitored to make sure that there is compliance. Sometimes the investigators recommend that a professor be demoted, lose tenure, or be terminated. This process may, however, take years.

SEXUAL HARASSMENT—WHAT ARE THE HIGH SCHOOLS DOING?

At this time, several school districts are in the process of writing procedures regarding sexual harassment policies for students, and faculty and staff. Some high schools are formulating a sexual harassment pamphlet.

Others, more typically, will place the information within the student handbook. Students who harass other students can be suspended. Teachers can be transferred or terminated, depending on the seriousness of the allegation.

Each district has a person who investigates complaints of sexual harassment or discrimination in general. If the matter is not settled within the school, by the principal, the district investigator steps in and makes recommendations. Sometimes a complaint is serious enough that it reaches the state department of education. The high school can lose educational funding if the matter is not resolved. The state may recommend that the teacher be terminated. Of course, if the harassment was on a physical level, the teacher will probably face criminal charges as well. Sexual harassment of a minor is a very serious matter.

WHAT A HIGH SCHOOL STUDENT SHOULD DO

High school students who feel they have been sexually harassed can take the following measures:

- Make sure to document what happened to you.

- Tell as many trusted people as possible—your parents, friends, the dean, the principal, other teachers—until the matter is resolved.

- If the matter is not taken seriously by the staff at your high school, contact the district person who investigates complaints of discrimination.

- You can also contact your state's department of education and wage a formal complaint.

- There are also legal remedies. Katy Lyle, for example, received $15,000 in the settlement of a sexual harassment case at Duluth Central High School, Minnesota.

SEXUAL HARASSMENT EDUCATION

Life Management Skills (LMS) is a course that is mandated by the Florida Department of Education. A little bit of everything is covered in the course, from balancing your checkbook to dealing with date and acquaintance rape. Sue Brown, an LMS teacher at Eastside High School in Gainesville, Florida, said:

> When the Clarence Thomas hearings were going on, we discussed sexual harassment. I found a quote by Clarence Thomas

and put it up on the board: 'You can make it but first you must endure.' This led to a discussion with the students. What about Anita Hill? Did she have to 'endure' in order to make it?

The LMS curriculum is constantly being re-evaluated and updated. Mrs. Mary Waters, Florida Department of Education, said, "Anyone can suggest what's included in the LMS curriculum. We send you a request form and you fill it out with your suggestion." More information on sexual harassment—what it is, how to recognize it, what you can do about it—will probably be more thoroughly covered in schools curricula in the future. Other states are also mandating curriculums similar to Florida's LMS.

LEGAL RECOURSE

You've tried all of the above and nothing satisfied you. The teacher continues to harass you. On Wednesday, February 26, 1992, the United States Supreme Court unanimously decided that students can collect money from schools in sexual harassment cases. Until this time, students who sought legal remedies could not get punitive and compensatory damages. They could only get the institution to change its policies.

For example, if a student sued because she was not allowed on the soccer team for gender reasons, the Court might rule that the school establish a girl's soccer team. Now that Title IX authorizes the award of monetary damages, more students may be seeking legal remedies, especially if the institution has been unresponsive to solving problems of sexual harassment.

ADVANTAGES OF SEEING AN ATTORNEY

There are several advantages to seeing an attorney, according to Lois Vanderwoerd, a St. Louis-based attorney and sexual harassment expert.

- Institutional panels at most institutions are very slow in making decisions. They take an inordinate amount of time to complete their investigations. The federal laws state that a complaint of sexual harassment must be filed within 180 days from the last incident of sexual harassment. (There are some deviations.)

- The attorney may be the only person who is truly rooting exclusively for you. People who work within an institution are often inclined to defend the hand that feeds them. The attorney knows the laws and will do his or her best to get the matter resolved in your favor. "The attorney only has loyalty to the student. A faculty person does not," Ms. Vanderwoerd said.

- If the student is looking to get monetary damages, he or she must see an attorney. None of the other remedies include monetary relief.

- The attorney can pressure the institution to expedite its decision and get the matter resolved more quickly than if a student approaches the administration by herself.

- A lawsuit may be the only way that the institution wakes up and starts being responsive to these matters

DRAWBACKS OF LEGAL RECOURSE

Going through the legal system doesn't guarantee a positive result every time. "A student who brings forth a case of sexual harassment against an institution is like David going up against Goliath," said Attorney Barbara Burkett, a sexual harassment expert in Gainesville, Florida. Other drawbacks include:

- Lack of witnesses. In order to win, the plaintiff needs to have good witnesses. "The administration is likely to isolate the victim. The teachers all know each other. They are on one side of the fence and the students are on the other. They will probably close ranks on the accused," Ms. Burkett said.

- Unless an attorney takes the case on a contingency fee basis, legal remedies can be very expensive.

- The victim will probably be branded as a trouble maker. A long, drawn-out legal battle, in which the victim is placed in the public eye, can be extremely stressful and painful for most victims.

- Monetary damages may be hard to prove. "If you complain and we first contact the institution, which is correct legal procedure, and they terminate the harasser, or fix your grade, or give you a psychologist, then what are your damages?" Ms. Burkett stated.

- The victim often becomes the accused. "Too often, the legal system falls prey to the mentality of questioning the victim instead of the authority figure," said Sarah Burns, National Council for Research on Women.

What Can We Expect in the Future?

Wouldn't it be nice if we were able to instantly recognize sexual harassers and avoid contact with them? Billie Wright Dziech, co-author of *The Lecherous Professor* (1990) with Linda Weiner attempted to profile the typical college professor harasser. Now, she feels she would eliminate the section which describes the typical harasser, if she revised the book.

"It is very difficult, if not impossible, to categorize the behaviors and to compose an adequate profile because there are many types of lecherous, sexist, and/or abusive individuals in our society."

One characteristic they have in common, according to Billie Wright Dziech, is their "awareness of vulnerabilities. They seem adept at spotting potential victims."

Dr. Dziech described the dilemma most institutions face regarding the issue of sexual harassment.

> There is a dual, complex problem. Institutions are obligated to look out for the institution, which means they are obligated to employees, faculty, and students. It's rather like a parent with a number of children whose interests conflict. Students' needs should be predominant, but institutions have other interests as well, such as the finances of the institution. If you are sued for a zillion dollars and you are a small school, then the interest of other students will suffer.

Most experts agree that greater institutional remedies are what is needed. "Because of the anguish that a legal course of action can cause victims of sexual harassment, the need for successful in-house intervention and resolution policies is crucial. However, studies show that institutional remedies do not measure up." (National Council for Research on Women 1991).

Perhaps, as more research is conducted on the long-term aftereffects of sexual harassment upon victims, more institutions will be motivated to take the issue as seriously as it is treated at Hunter College. "I don't believe it is possible to overstate the influence that a major advisor can have on the life of a person he chooses to harass; there have been suicides because of it," says Anne Truax, from the University of Minnesota and the National Council for Research on Women.

SUMMARY

Sexual harassment is no joking matter. If you perceive yourself as a victim of sexual harrassment, do not wait to take measures that can remedy the situation. A victim is someone who is powerless to affect their situation. Take action—remember the four ways to deal with sexual harassment:

1. Individual recourse

2. Institutional recourse

3. Federal recourse

4. Legal recourse

A U.S. New and World Report article, "Sex in America," (Schrof and Wagner 1994) said:

> . . . In general, researchers have found that men are more prone than women to read sexual implications into casual encounters. That may explain the results of a University of New Orleans study that found men thought women had initiated sexual encounters in far more instances than the women themselves said they had. "The survey shows how troubled the relationship between the sexes still is," says Gagnon, because the signals men and women are trying to send each other often get confused.

Confused signals result from poor communication. Developing good communication skills is ultimately one of the best defenses against sexual harassment.

All the stories are true and come from real people. I asked students at a large, southern public university and at a small, northern private college to submit their stories to me. Names have been changed but the information is true according to those who submitted their stories.

Appendix

Power in Numbers

Throughout this book it was stated that students can get more accomplished if they work as part of a team. Here are organizations you can join on the high school and college level to help affect change.

COLLEGE ORGANIZATIONS

For college students, there are fraternities, sororities, clubs, and student government. Fraternities, sororities, and clubs give students an opportunity to socialize and to learn which professors are the best and the worst. Often, the students in fraternal organizations share class notes with one another. Sometimes free tutoring and counseling is available.

Student governments usually have more political power than fraternal organizations. The following interview with a student government president will give you a general idea of what student government can offer you.

ALEX PATTON, PAST PRESIDENT (1993)
STUDENT GOVERNMENT, UNIVERSITY OF FLORIDA
GAINESVILLE, FL

> We have two different avenues for students who have problems with teachers: (1) We have a specific cabinet called the Student Advocacy Cabinet which is there to help students appeal grades and communicate better with difficult teachers. Students can come in and complain about teachers or just complain in general,

such as bureaucratic red tape or not knowing how to get something done and this cabinet will hopefully get something done.

Here's an example. Let's say there's a problem with a teacher and a grade. The student would contact the Student Advocacy Cabinet. The Cabinet would listen to the problem and then, depending upon the nature of the problem, they might recommend that we take the problem directly to the provost. What happens next depends on the situation, but once the provost office gets involved, things usually are done.

It's tough at a large university. You can feel like you're being swallowed up and you're just a social security number. But usually if you're persistent you'll reach your goal in whatever you're trying to accomplish.

HIGH SCHOOL ORGANIZATIONS

Let's say that a high school student has had a problem with a teacher and he's done everything this book has so far recommended; he's talked with the teacher, the dean, the school principal. Maybe his parents even went so far as to contact the board of education and nothing worked. Outside of legal remedies, what else can the student do? There are two other solutions. First, the student could contact government representatives, such as senators and congressmen.

But there is one more option available to high school students with special problems. There is a handful of nonprofit organizations in the United States that receive funding and donations to help students who have been treated unfairly by the system. These organizations are members of a larger organization called the National Coalition of Advocates for Students (NCAS). NCAS does not help students directly, but it helps the organizations that are committed to helping students. The NCAS mission statement says:

NCAS began in 1975 as a voluntary network of education advocates concerned about rising suspension and expulsion rates in public schools. Since then, NCAS has grown into a national advocacy organization with 23 member groups in 14 states.

NCAS works to achieve equal access to a quality public education for vulnerable students, particularly those who are poor, children of color, recently immigrated, or differently-abled.

Rooted in the civil rights movement of the 1960s, NCAS reflects 25 years of advocacy experience on the part of its member groups.

Focusing on kindergarten through grade 12, NCAS informs and mobilizes citizens and policymakers to help resolve critical education issues. Utilizing national projects and studies, public hearings, and outreach through publications and the news media, NCAS raises concerns that might otherwise not be heard.

I contacted several of the NCAS member groups and interviewed directors. The following interviews will give you a better understanding of the issues that NCAS groups deal with, in case you feel you ever need to contact the one nearest you. (My questions appear in italics.)

BOB SCHWARTZ, DIRECTOR
JUVENILE LAW CENTER
PHILADELPHIA, PA

The Juvenile Law Center is a nonprofit public interest law firm which advances the rights of children involved with public agencies, by working for the reform and coordination of the child welfare, juvenile justice, mental health, and public health care systems.

EMILY BUSS, DEPUTY DIRECTOR,
JUVENILE LAW CENTER,
PHILADELPHIA, PA

Our aim is to focus on minimization and inappropriate state intrusion on kids' and families' lives. And to help kids and families get services that are home based and community based whenever possible. We get a lot of calls from kids and from lawyers and parents—everything from where to go (when a kid wants to leave an abusive situation) to where to go to school.

What would you recommend if the student feels he received an unfair grade?

We'd probably tie him into the Education Law Center in Philadelphia. If, on the other hand, he's trying to live independently because his parents are drug addicts and he can't switch schools because it's not in the district where his parents live, then we can help. We can also help the child who is emancipated.

LOLA GLOVER, DIRECTOR
COALITION FOR QUALITY EDUCATION
TOLEDO, OHIO

What kinds of issues have you handled regarding difficult teachers and students?

There are two incidents that come to mind. The first involved a special education teacher. He made the girls sit up front, unbutton their blouses, and then he drew their breasts on the board. We went to the principal, to no avail. Then we went to the central administration. The children's claims were not taken seriously, but we believed the children. So, we got a van and filled it with parents and we went to the central administration every day for five days. We demanded a room, a pot of coffee and someone to meet with us who would have some voice over what was going on. And we wrote a letter every day about our experience.

The system here has gotten a lot better now. In the past the philosophy was, 'We won't allow parents or outside groups tell us what to do or how to do it.' But we followed this case very closely and demanded that he be ousted as a teacher. At first they just shipped him to another school, but we kept persisting and he was eventually fired. We never went through legal procedures because we felt that the students had already been through enough.

The second incident involved segregated classes. We called on the NAACP and we got it straightened out. These were complaints by parents. Students complain more about the treatment they get from teachers as far as being disrespectful to them, trumping up charges to suspend them, or treating them unfairly. We got a lot of complaints about unfairness.

What would you recommend if a student feels he received a vendetta grade?

My recommendation would be that anytime a student has a problem, we need to let him know there is recourse. Talk to parents or some other adult.

Ms. Glover emphasized how important it is to teach students how to document. "We need to teach parents and kids documentation.

They shouldn't just talk verbally. Put everything in writing—everything that was told to the teachers and administrators—everyone. And make sure that not only does the administration have a copy, but also the central administration, the principal, and the board of education members. Everything that transpired between the student and the teacher needs to be documented.

When we can't get results on the school level, we get the best responses from the central administration when we document everything. We need to teach kids their rights and we need to teach them to *document*. It makes a *big* difference. If you just argue about it and talk about it on the phone, nothing gets done. But once its in writing, it becomes the *facts*. People will now begin to look at it. And school boards don't want that kind of stuff floating around because you can also send that documentation to your state legislature.

So, have kids sit down and write. That's my strongest recommendation. We need to teach our children how to write and document what has truly happened to them. Once we put something in writing, people are going to read it and its not over until it's settled—even if we have to go to the state legislature with it.

ELENA SILVA, ASSISTANT TO
THE DIRECTOR OF LEADERSHIP
AND COMMUNITY SERVICE
ASPIRA ASSOCIATION, INC.
WASHINGTON, D.C.

We deal specifically with Latino students. Our efforts lean mostly toward leadership development and education. But we also conduct research and we inform policy makers on issues that are most critical to Latinos. We have offices in Puerto Rico and in six other states. The associate offices deal directly with the students. There are school clubs and ASPIRA organizations that deal within the schools. It's basically to advance the development of the Latino community in general and give them opportunities to continue their education.

If a student was having a problem with a teacher, we would refer them to speak with the school board. We would then refer them to our organization that deals with legal matters. We could not do anything personally if a student was having a hard time with a difficult teacher. We would just refer them.

STEVE BING, DIRECTOR
MASSACHUSETTS ADVOCACY CENTER
BOSTON, MASSACHUSETTS

Parents are usually the ones to call us. They learn about our organization through word of mouth. Our main issues are school suspensions and expulsions and special education. We don't get into marginal issues because we just don't have the resources.

If a student was suspended, we try to ensure that the rules were followed and then we also try to get him back in school as soon as possible.

If there is an actual expulsion (where the student is terminated from school permanently—this is becoming kind of an epidemic), then we try to find an alternative education program.

We have this new school expulsion law in Massachusetts which makes it very easy to expel kids. There are three offenses for which a school principal can expel: (1) possession of an illegal substance, (2) possession of a dangerous weapon, and (3) assault on staff (physical).

It used to be school committees that made the expulsion decision, but now it's the principals, which makes it a lot easier for the principal, *plus*, the new law says to principals that if you *don't* expel, you have to explain why. The students do not have to be mandatory school age. We've had kids as young as eight years old who have been permanently expelled. No alternative education has to be provided for them, according to the new law. It's mandatory that children attend school; however, it's not mandatory that schools provide children an opportunity to attend school. The law says that if a child is expelled, there is no statutory obligation to provide alternative education, even if the child is 16.

So, what does your organization do?

First of all, we try to get them back in school. It's a very complex process. It's a brand new law and we're also looking at ways to litigate whether or not the law is constitutional. We've had several expulsion cases ranging from possession of marijuana to possession of a knife. We haven't represented anybody who walked into school with a gun, although I suspect that'll happen soon.

What would you like kids to know who read this book?

They should know their rights, especially in the areas of suspension and expulsion. They should clearly know what are the offenses for which that can be the punishment. And schools should have an obligation—I think that's clear under the law— to give kids notice of the behavior that's expected of them.

What could I expect from local school administrators if I wanted to start a group such as yours in my area?

Hostility. Schools are probably the most conservative institution that children encounter. They're hard to change. They're very set in their ways. And they don't like outside interference. We've been around since 1969. We receive our funding from foundations, and every year it gets harder to raise funding. The less new you are, the less attractive you are to a foundation. Foundations like to fund high impact, high visibility organizations.

What do you think about corporal punishment for students?

I cannot believe that anyone thinks it's a good idea. But they do. What we're saying, in effect, is "We want you to be nonviolent and nice, but if you do something we don't like, we're going to smack you." That to me is the supreme stupid message. There's only one that's more stupid—schools suspend students for being truant. It doesn't make sense. "If you don't want to come to school, we won't let you." That seems pretty silly.

DIANA AUTIN, DIRECTOR
ADVOCATES FOR CHILDREN OF NEW YORK
LONG ISLAND CITY, NY

Funded by foundations, Advocates for Children of New York works at helping keep children in school. The organization receives government contracts to work with children who have been placed in foster homes. In addition, they hold classes for parents in education law and advocacy techniques. "We give parents both legal information and practical strategies for resolving school-related problems," explained Director Diana Autin. Their clients are obtained mainly from parents' organizations, such as United Parents Association. They train about 4,000 parents per year. To help their clients as best as possible, members of their staff speak a variety of foreign languages—English, Spanish, Haitian, and Chinese.

Most of the problems the staff hears are related to students being placed in special education classes or being suspended. For example: a student brought a box cutter to school that he used in an afterschool job. The chancellor instituted a policy of mandatory expulsion for any student who brought any kind of weapon to school, so the student—an Afro-American—was expelled, even though he was unaware of the policy and had proof that the box cutter was used in his job.

When Advocates for Children of New York became involved in the case they discovered two important things: (1) the rule of automatic expultion for possession of a weapon was being applied almost exclusively to only Afro-American males, and (2) "We found a part of the state law that said that students of compulsory attendance age can't be suspended to nowhere," said Ms. Autin. "You have to take into consideration the student's prior disciplinary record and you have to provide the student with appropriate alternative instruction. So we brought up these issues to the commissioner and we got the policy overturned and the student reinstated."

The student himself was unaware of his rights. By getting the experts at Advocates for Children involved, he was able to resume attending classes.

Another example of how Advocates for Children of New York helps children involves a case in which a teacher claimed that a kindergartener assaulted him. "This kindergartener," said Ms. Autin, "is very slight and small—about three feet tall—and the teacher is about a 260 pound male." The alleged assault occurred when the teacher would not permit the student to go to the lavaratory because it was not recess time.

> And the kid was flailing because the teacher was restraining him. It was an Afro-American kindergartener and it was a white male teacher. And the principal wanted the student transferred out of the school. So, we went to the suspension hearing and we said this was not an assault. This should never have been treated as a superintendent suspension hearing. The child is a kindergartener, for God's sake, and you're going to take the kid away from his neighborhood school and send him someplace else because he flailed a 260 pound teacher who was keeping him from going to the bathroom!? We got the charges dismissed and the student reinstated.

Ms. Autin recommended that students become as informed as possible about their rights withing the school system. Many school districts have little booklets about *Your Rights and Responsibilities as a Student.* Students can also request the information from their school principal or superintendant.

I would also recommend that students enlist, as much as possible, the support of their parents. In addition to whatever rights the students have, the parents also have additional rights.

I would also recommend the students seek out the assistance of anyone in their school who they feel is understanding and could be an ally on their side because there are times when an insider can apply friendly persuasion to their colleagues to resolve a situation.

And finally, if all else fails, I would recommend that students and their parents try to see if there are local or statewide organizations that can help. There are two places they can contact if they don't know of anything in their own locality. First, they could contact the National Coalition of Advocates for Students who has a list of NCAS and other similar kinds of organizations that help students. (100 Boylston Street, Suite 737; Boston, Massachusetts 02116; Phone: (617) 357-8507, Fax: (617) 357-9549). Or they can call us, Advocates for Children of New York, Long Island City, New York at (718) 729-8866. We'll try to find organizations that can help them in their locality.

There are other organizations in the United States that are designed to help teenagers with a variety of problems, including problems they may face at school. H.I.T.T., for example, based in Gainesville, Florida is the Hippodrome Improvisational Teen Theatre. Each year, teens are selected to be a part of the core group of performers. Together, they write and dramatize true life scripts about provocative subjects such as AIDS, teen pregnancy, divorcing parents, abuse, drugs, intimate relationships, and problems with teachers. The teens perform at local high schools and after the performance, discussion is generated. None of the skits show solutions to the problems. That's what the after-performance discussion is for. The teens also make it clear that solutions are not universally applicable to everyone.

Runaway shelters, located across the nation, represent yet another organization that is very supportive of teenagers.

MARIA BAXTER, COUNSELOR
INTERFACE SHELTER
GAINESVILLE, FL

Kids can only stay with us six months. If there is a problem in the school we let the parents do the intervention. We don't touch it. If the kid is in foster care then HRS does the interventions. So we don't really get involved. What we do with kids who are having conflict in their life, be it school, parents, any conflict, we teach them conflict resolution skills. We teach them how to negotiate around the problem rather than use violent tactics. We teach them communication skills to ask for what they want and to negotiate what they want, respecting that everybody has needs. The training is either one on one or maybe there is a group of children who need the skill and then we make it part of the life skill program.

What would you recommend to children having problems with teachers?

I would tell them to go to their parents and ask them to help intervene. Parents really need to be involved in the school system. When the parents aren't involved, I think that's when kids have trouble in school. If their parents are not supportive then they need to go to their guidance counselor at the school and see if they can get the guidance counselor to assist. And if that fails then they need to reach the principal, and if that fails, then they're in trouble because there's very little that can be done. A kid really has no power. The system is so powerful. A kid can yell and scream that the teacher is unfair but the principal, the system, is going to protect itself. I stress the parents' intervention because without the parents the kids have very little power. The only system that can be more powerful than the educational system is the family system. I feel very strongly about that. Very strongly. If the kid doesn't have the protection of the parent in the school system, the kid is liable to be a victim of it.

JIM HIGHT, PUBLISHER
UNITED YOUTH MAGAZINE
BOSTON, MA
ALSO: HEAD OF UNITED YOUTH OF BOSTON AND THE TEEN INITIATES PROJECT

We give out small grants to teenagers who are doing something in their neighborhoods. *United Youth* is a magazine and writing program where teenagers write about the issues that affect them. We just had a special issue where students wrote about their problems with teachers.

The special issue came as a result of a day long workshop at Madison Park High School. The school closed for a day on June 10, 1993—known as Institute Day. Students and teachers gathered for the day to discuss problems that the school faces and examine what could be done. For instance, one of the problems mentioned was a teacher who does not approve of Mr. Hight's magazine. He calls it "Nazi literature" because the magazine runs ads for birth control. Many issues were discussed and it was a good beginning.

I'd like to see more of these days every day at school. And I'd like to see common goals for change that students, teachers, and administrators can agree upon.

MAURA WOLF, DIRECTOR
TEENS AS COMMUNITY RESOURCES
BOSTON, MA

We help students mobilize around community or school issues that they feel is important to them.

How do you find your students?

Wide outreach through mailings, mouth-to-mouth, mail outs to young people who have worked with us in the past and youth organizations in the schools.

If there was a serious problem at a school involving a difficult teacher, Ms. Wolf says she would help the teenagers to first talk about the problem and then to organize a group and form a coalition or write a petition or organize a project. She also was involved in a day-long workshop where teens, teachers, and administrators came together to discuss and solve problems.

It was called the Youth Mobilization Project and it actually was a year long project. We basically took over the school for a day. We got everyone's view on problems. It was co-facilitated by students who are part of Teens as Community Resources. Here were some of the recommendations:

• Create a teacher evaluation process using student input.

• Provide students with the necessary information to meet requirements and be successful.

- Provide child care so students can finish school.

- Learn more about the history of nonwhite people.

- Provide more hands-on learning.

- Have a better grievance process and guarantee that administrators will listen to the students.

There's now a task force that's working on these issues and a school committee that's looking at restructuring.

How did the faculty take to you doing this?

I think initially a couple of teachers really pushed for it. But there were others who weren't very excited and questioned the academic value of taking a day to do this. Even after the day passed, some felt it was a wonderful opportunity to engage in dialogue and some did not.

Part of the requirement of the Perkins Act—an act that mandates that vocational education needs to go through a major restructuring—mandates student involvement and student input, so the Boston school system paid for this. It was their way of meeting this requirement. It's exciting and a lot of people are still hoping and waiting to see how it gets implemented. The majority of kids in city schools are not receiving the education that they deserve or need. I don't believe student rights are supported very much.

What other kinds of issues does Teens as Community Resources try to solve?

There was a group of inner-city teens who came to us and complained that they had no space for congregating. So, we helped them write a grant to create youth council. Now they meet once a week in the basement of a church for recreational games and socializing. They have their own turf.

So what advice would you give to students reading this book?

Don't underestimate the power and the responsibilities you have. Speak up and challenge people. And you should work with people to change the things you don't think are right.

Ms. JANEL PARKER, ENRICHMENT MANAGER
BOSTON PARTNERS IN EDUCATION
BOSTON, MA

Their brochure states,

Boston Partners in Education is a nonprofit multicultural agency dedicated to supporting the academic growth and social development of public school children. Linking a wide variety of community resources to schools, BPE provides programs and services to teachers, students, administrators, and parents.

Do you have a mediator on staff in case there is a dispute between a teacher and a student?

A student wouldn't contact us directly. The teacher or an administrator would contact this agency. We have afterschool programs and boys' and girls' clubs. We help schools find career speakers. We have a psychologist on board who is a consultant for us. Her name is Dr. Lonnie Cardin and she has a TV and radio program. As a last resort we'd ask her to be a mediator.

We recruit, train, and place 4,000 volunteers in the Boston public schools every year. And we work essentially from teachers' and principals' requests. If they need something special they fill out one of our forms and we do our best. If they want a reading lab program we will more than likely pair up a bank that's near the school and send readers every week. If we get some volunteer who comes in who has an unusual quality, like an attorney who also has a rock and roll band who wants to show kids how they can start a rock band, we would then call a school we knew that has a good music program and we'd speak to the music teachers and say, "Would you like someone to come and tell your students how to set up a rock band?" If a student called with a request for something along these lines we'd say, "Sure. But have your teacher or principal fill out one of our forms."

We are part of a national program. We have a Washington office. There are these organizations all over the country. They used to be called School Volunteers for (you name your city). But some of the organizations have changed into Partners in Education. We get a small amount of funding from the school department and largely by writing proposals and grants constantly and from contributions.

SUMMARY

The purpose of this appendix is to share with you some of the organized resources that are available to you if you need support in dealing with difficult teachers, or school related problems, or if you want to get something accomplished. Some of the organizations listed in this chapter may not exist in your area. My advice to you is to be proactive. Consider starting such a group if you feel there is a need in your community. For funding, try foundations. I am told that attorneys are another good resource. Not only may some attorneys help to fund your start-up effort, but they may also be willing to help if an issue arises that requires legal intervention. Send letters to 500 attorneys. Ask for donations and even if 10% contribute, you'll have your seed money to get started.

We need a strong system of checks and balances to make sure that everyone in our educational system has a voice.

One last suggestion. Another way to be heard is to write a play. A number of years ago, I wrote a musical comedy, *The Last of the True Scholars*, which dramatizes, in part, my experiences with graduate school. (Please write me if you are interested in obtaining a copy of the script). Changes can be made when students dramatize the problems they face.

Throughout this book, I have provided you with information that is not readily available elsewhere and may run counter to the myths you have heard regarding higher education. I welcome you to contact me if you are interested in starting a peer mediation program in your school, or if you are interested in a day-long workshop. I'm always interested in hearing your comments and feedback.

—Dr. Angela V. Woodhull
Soulutions Seminars
P.O. Box 14423
Gainesville, FL 32604–2423

Bibliography

Abbey, Antonia. "Sex Differences in Attributions for Friendly Behavior: Do Males Misperceive Females' Friendliness? *Journal of Personality and Social Psychology*, vol. 42, no. 5, pp. 830–838. The American Psychological Association, Inc.

Abel, Emily K. 1984. *Terminal Degrees: The Job Crisis in Higher Education*. New York: Praeger Publishers.

Associated Press. 1985. "Prof's Killer Set Free, Refuses to Express Remorse," *Gainesville Sun*, 9 September, p. 5C.

———. 1987. "Prospects Bright for College Grads," *Gainesville Sun*, 19 December, p. 1.

———. 1995. "Colleges Fudged Figures for Magazine Rankings," *Gainesville Sun*, 18 April, pp. 1A and 9A.

Bergen, Jane. 1986. *Robots in the Classroom: A Look at the American Educational Factory*. Wolfe City, Tex.: Henington Publishing Company.

Betz, Nancy E. and Louise F. Fitzgerald. 1987. *The Career Psychology of Women*, San Diego, CA: Academic Press. Reprint in Michele A. Paludi and Richard Barickman. 1992. *Academic and Workplace Sexual Harassment*. Albany, N.Y.: SUNY Press.

Carnegie, Dale. 1982. *How to Win Friends and Influence People*. Revised and edited by Arthur R. Pell. New York: Pocket Books, A division of Simon & Schuster.

DeBlieu, Jan. 1984. "The Business of Student Recruiting," *Emory Magazine.* February, pp. 14–19.

Dziech, Billie Wright and Linda Weiner. 1990. *The Lecherous Professor.* 2nd ed. Champaign, Ill.: University of Illinois Press.

Glaser, R. and J. Thorpe. 1986. "Unethical Intimacy: A Survey of Sexual Contact and Advances between Psychology Educators and Female Graduate Students. *American Psychologist,* 41. pp. 43–51.

Goldberg, Herb and George R. Bach. 1974. *Creative Aggression.* New York: Avon Books.

Hall, Roberta M. and Bernice R. Sandler. 1982. "The Classroom Climate: A Chilly One for Women?" The Project on the Status and Education of Women of the Association of American Colleges.

Hill, John. 1995. "There Are No More Dream Careers," *Gainesville Sun.* 25 June.

Horn, Jack. 1986. *Supervisor's Factomatic.* Englewood Cliffs, N.J.: Prentice Hall.

Hughey, James D. and Bena Harper. 1983. "What's In a Grade?" ERIC, ED 248549.

Hunter College. 1990. Sexual Harass*ment: Myths and Realities.* New York: Hunter College. Based on Jean O. Hughes and Bernice R. Sandler. *In Case of Sexual Harassment: A Guide for Women Students.* A publication of the Project on the Status and Education of Women, Association of American Colleges, Washington D.C.

Keen, Larry. 1984. "UF Registar: Humanites are Protected," *Gainesville Sun,* 1 December.

Littwin, Susan. 1986. *The Postponed Generation.* New York: William Morrow and Company.

London, Dean Herbert. 1987. "Death of the University," *The Futurist.* May–June.

Lowerberg, Peter. 1983. *Decoding the Past*. New York: Knopf.

Magrin, Jud. 1992. "UF Grad Student Claims Sexual Harassment," *Gainesville Sun*, 2 April, pp. 1B and 2B.

McGahey, Richard. 1990. "Job Market Tight for New Grads," *Social Justice Review*. March–April, p. 77.

Nasrin, Jenab. 1989. "Survey—Freshmen Enter College to Get Better Jobs," *Chronicle of Higher Education*. September.

National Council for Research on Women. 1991. *Sexual Harassment: Research and Resources*. November. Washington, D.C.

Norris, Emma Coburn. 1985. "College and The American Dream," *Chronicle of Higher Education*, 17 July.

Paludi, Michele A., editor. 1990. *Ivory Power: Sexual Harassment on Campus*. Albany, N.Y.: SUNY Press.

Paludi, Michele A. and Richard Barickman. 1992. *Academic and Workplace Sexual Harassment*. Albany, NY: SUNY Press.

Ridgeway, James. 1968. *The Closed Corporation: American Universities in Crisis*. New York: Random House.

Ross, Victor J. and John Marlowe. 1985. *The Forbidden Apple: Sex in the Schools*. Palm Springs, Calif.: ETC Publications.

Rowe, Mary P. 1981. "Dealing with Sexual Harassment," *Harvard Business Review*. May–June.

Rumberger, Russell W. 1982. *The Structure of Work and the Underutilization of College-Educated Workers*. Report No. IFG–PR–82–B7.

———. 1983. *Education, Unemployment and Productivity*. Report No. 83–A14.

———. 1984. *High Technology and Job Loss*. Report No. 84–A12.

Rumberger, Russell W. and Henry M. Levin. 1984. *Forecasting the Impact of New Technologies on the Future Job Market*. Report No. 84–A4.

Seagrave, Jane (Associated Press). 1985. "Group Therapy May be Cure for Ph.D. Blues," *Gainesville Sun*, 19 February, p. 1A.

Schrof, Joannie M., and Betsy Wagner. 1994. "Sex in America," *U.S. News & World Report*, October 17, p.78.

Sexual Harassment Panel of Hunter College. 1990. *Sexual Harassment on Campus is a Problem: You Can Stop It*. New York: Hunter College. Based on information from the following sources; Nancy Bailey and Margaret Richards: "Tarnishing the ivory tower: Sexual harassment in graduate training programs in psychology." (Paper presented at the American Psychological Association, Los Angeles, Calif., 1985.)

Meg Bond: "Division 27 sexual harassment survey: Definition, impact, and environmental context." (*The Community Psychologist*, 1988, 21,7–10.)

Louise Fitzgerald, Sandra Shullman, Nancy Bailey, Margaret Richards, Janice Swecker, Yael Gold, Mimi Ormerod and Lauren Weitzman: "The incidence and dimensions of sexual harassment in academia and the workplace." (*Journal of Vocational Behavior*, 1988, 32, 152–175.)

Sommers, Robert. 1990. "Educators: College Not Just Preparation for Job," *Independent Florida Alligator*.

Stock, Pamela. 1995. "Work Q & A," *Mademoiselle*. May. p. 92.

Sykes, Charles J. 1988. *Profscam: Professors and the Demise of Higher Education*. Washington, D.C.: Regenry Gateway.

Till, Frank J. 1980. "Sexual Harassment: A Report on the Sexual Harassment of Student," The National Advisory Council on Women's Educational Programs. August. Washington, D.C.

Weisberg, Jacob. 1993. "Useless U?" *Mademoiselle*. August, pp. 148–151.

Wolfe, Tom. 1973. "The Feature Game," *The New Journalism*. New York: Harper and Row, pp. 3–4.

————. 1990. "Should You Send Your Child to College?" *Social Justice Review*, March–April, pp. 76–81.

Yardley, Jonathan, 1984. "Translated, This Jargon Says Our Colleges are Dreadful," *The Washington Post National Weekly Edition*, 19 November, p. 24.